D0020048

CHRISTIAN
ETHICS

Abingdon Essential Guides
Editorial Advisory Board

Nancy T. Ammerman
Hartford Seminary

Don S. Browning
University of Chicago Divinity School

Rebecca S. Chopp
Candler School of Theology

Justo L. González
Emory University

Walter J. Harrelson
Vanderbilt University Divinity School

E. Brooks Holifield
Candler School of Theology

George G. Hunter
Asbury Theological Seminary

Allan Kirton
The United Methodist Mission Resource Center

Jane Dammen McAuliffe
University of Toronto

Peter J. Paris
Princeton Theological Seminary

Orlo Strunk, Jr.
The Journal of Pastoral Care

CHRISTIAN ETHICS

An Essential Guide

Robin W. Lovin

ABINGDON PRESS
Nashville

BJ1251
.L69
2000

CHRISTIAN ETHICS: AN ESSENTIAL GUIDE

Copyright © 2000 by Abingdon Press

All rights reserved. # 4339089 7

No part of this work may be reproduced or transmitted in any form or by any means, electronic or mechanical, including photocopying and recording, or by means of any information storage or retrieval system, except as may be expressly permitted by the 1976 Copyright Act or in writing from the publisher. Requests for permission should be addressed to Abingdon Press, 201 Eighth Avenue South, Nashville, TN 37202-0801.

This book is printed on recycled, acid-free paper.

Library of Congress Cataloging-in-Publication Data

Lovin, Robin W., 1946-
    Christian Ethics: an essential guide / Robin W. Lovin.
      p.   cm.—(Abingdon essential guides)
    Includes bibliographical references and index.
    ISBN 0-687-05462-1 (alk. paper)
      1. Christian Ethics.   I. Title.   II. Series.
    BJ1251 .L69   2000   00-021985
    241—dc21   CIP

Scripture quotations, unless otherwise indicated, are from the New Revised Standard Version Bible, copyright © 1989, by the Division of Christian Education of the National Council of the Churches of Christ in the United States of America.

Scripture quotations marked KJV are from the King James Version of the Bible.

00 01 02 03 04 05 06 07 08 09—10 9 8 7 6 5 4 3 2 1

MANUFACTURED IN THE UNITED STATES OF AMERICA

Contents

Preface

Ethics is a slightly mysterious subject to most people. Even those with a good deal of education may not have studied it directly, the way they once took courses in chemistry or literature. When journalists and commentators and members of Congress start talking about ethics, it is usually a warning that something has gone badly wrong. When we hear that an ethics committee is looking into someone's conduct, we do not assume that the investigation is because this person is being considered for an award for exemplary ethical behavior.

Yet ethics, in the original understanding of the term, is basically about the positive goals and directions we all set for our lives. Ethics is about how we try to become good people and shape for ourselves a life that is worth living.

For Christians, that effort cannot be separated from what we believe about God and about our relationship to God. Faith and ethics are inextricably linked, though not always in the simple way that we think when we try to please God by being good.

For the past two decades I've been a teacher of ethics, mostly to women and men who were studying to be ordained ministers or scholars of theology, but also to people of all ages in church classrooms, professional seminars, lunchtime discussion groups, and continuing education programs. Often it is the most elementary teaching that is the most difficult because it involves sorting out some ways of thinking about the good life that are so familiar to us that we do not always realize we are thinking about it at all. There are no predetermined methods to be taught and no set answers to be learned. That is not because there are no right answers, but because it is in the nature of ethics that unless you come to the right answer for yourself, it is not really a moral choice.

Those of us who teach ethics have to learn to accept the fact that in this course everyone really does know the subject before the class begins.

Still, there are some questions that need to be asked and some things we can learn from the experience of those who have gone before us.

This book is an attempt to share some of those questions and experiences with a wider audience. I appreciate especially the help of those who listened to me talk about these ideas while I was also trying to write about them: adult classes at First United Methodist Church, Highland Park United Methodist Church, and Northaven United Methodist Church in Dallas, Texas; Laity Week seminars in Dallas and in Anchorage, Alaska; and the local pastors in the Course of Study School at Perkins School of Theology. I am grateful to faculty colleagues and to my administrative assistant, Sue Ferrell, who helped me make the time to bring this project to completion, and especially to Chad Wilkes, who helped with the research, editing, and notes.

Robin W. Lovin
Dallas, Texas
July, 1999

CHAPTER 1

Choices

Everyone wants to have a good life. Aristotle (384–322 BC), the Greek philosopher who gave us Western civilization's first systematic treatise on ethics, thought that everything we do aims at some good. Ethics is the study of that human good in its most general terms and how we human beings pursue it.[1] Because all of us *are* pursuing it, one way or another, ethics is a subject in which almost everyone is interested.

For many Christians living twenty-three centuries later, Aristotle's view still seems to fit our situation pretty well. Thinking about how to live a good life occupies a lot of our time and attention. We seek satisfying and enduring personal relationships with people who enjoy sharing the same activities we enjoy. We want to build comfortable homes and secure futures for our families. We try to do good work and advance in our careers. Because we know that a good life is not built on material things alone, we also think about improving our health and expanding our minds. We try to figure out whether the entertainment we watch and the products we buy belong in a good life. We worry about how the emotions we feel on the job and the things we sometimes have to do to get our jobs done relate to a good life. We think about people whose faces we see in the newspaper or on television, people whose lives have been shaken by war or violence or natural disasters, and we wonder how their needs relate to our lives.

As Christians, we learn much of what we know about the good life through participation in churches and through personal prayer and Bible study. We take many of our images and the language of our questions from the Bible, especially from Jesus' parables and lessons in the New Testament. We wonder whether we pay enough attention to people in need, whether they are around the corner or on the other side of the world, to live up to the ideal of compassion that we learn from the story of the good Samaritan (Luke 10:29-37). We worry that we may become like the rich fool who built new barns to hold the abundance of his goods, but couldn't see the poverty in his relationship to God (Luke 12:13-21). We would rather be like Mary, who knew what was really important, than like Martha, who exhausted herself trying to do too many things at once (Luke 10:38-42). We try to sort out our obligations, and we wonder whether we are really giving Caesar what belongs to Caesar and giving God what belongs to God (Luke 20:20-26).

We think a lot about how to live good lives, and we worry a lot about the commitments and conflicts that get in the way of living well. Although our concerns are often voiced in specifically Christian language, we know that this search for inner peace, integrity in relationships, and genuine care for other people is widely shared by our neighbors, whether or not they share our Christian faith. Over coffee breaks at work, in parents' discussions at the public school, or just across the back fence on a weekend afternoon, we learn that the search for a good life is going on all around us. Increasingly, as travel, communication, and commerce shrink the globe and bring us into contact with people our grandparents never knew, we find that the questions that perplex us are being asked, perhaps in somewhat different ways, by people everywhere. Aristotle's ancient notion that seeking the good is something we all do seems to hold up well across the changes of history and the differences of culture.

Trying to live a good life is something that nearly everybody does. What they disagree about is what makes a life good.

What Is a Good Life?

For some, trying to live a good life means primarily seeking what popular culture would call "the good life," a life built around pleasant and interesting experiences, with enough money and leisure so that you can choose what to do for yourself. Perhaps, too, this good life includes access to places and events that are "exclusive," that many people want, but only a few can enjoy.

While many people daydream about such a life, those who actually pursue it learn very quickly that even a life of pleasure requires self-restraint and discipline. Some pleasures damage health and produce more pain over the long run, and even innocent amusements become unpleasant or boring when indulged to excess. Living a good life seems to require more than just seeking the next good experience.

More important, we quickly discover that even as we are trying to live a good life, there are many other people around us trying to do the same thing. Sometimes we limit our pursuit of things that are good for us in order to make the good life possible for them too. Parents often give up their own pleasures to make their children's lives richer, and spouses make sacrifices in their careers to enable their partner to pursue education or job possibilities. Consumers worry, appropriately, about whether the products they purchase are made by exploiting children or abusing animals, especially when those products are luxury items they could do without.

At first, this willingness to restrain pursuit of the good for oneself in order to make a good life possible for others may appear to be little more than a form of self-interest: helping others in the hope that they will help me, or at least ensuring that they will not actively oppose my aims. But it also rests on the recognition that helping others to live good lives is a part of what living the good life is. We would not think that we were living a good life if we had all the things and experiences we wanted, but were regarded by everyone around us as selfish and uncaring. Once we have achieved even a little security in our own lives, knowing that we have done things that made better lives for other people becomes an increasingly important part of living a good life.

Living a good life requires us to do some things to make our own lives good, but it also involves us in relationships that may require us to choose against what is most obviously good for ourselves. Striking the right balance here is no easy matter. If we follow a simple rule, like "Always think of other people first," we may do a lot of good for other people; but we may never develop the skills, wealth, and knowledge that would enable us to help them even more. We may even wear ourselves out in the effort, so that in the end we do not do as much for others by thinking about them all the time as we would if we thought a little more about ourselves. Appropriate self-concern is difficult to measure, however, and given the chance, we are apt to reward ourselves with more than we strictly need in order to sustain our efforts on behalf of others.

Living a good life is far more complex than either always choosing the things that advance our own interests or always putting other people first. What the good life requires of us probably cannot be reduced to a simple rule, but one thing is clear: Sometimes living a good life will mean giving up what is obviously and immediately good for us in order to do something that makes a good life possible for others.

The Good Life and the Christian Life

Few thoughtful people try to live a good life on entirely selfish terms, and most of our neighbors of other faiths or no faith would agree that the good life must include a concern for the good lives of others. For Christians, however, this general understanding is sharpened by the teachings and example of Jesus. Jesus often takes generally accepted obligations and pushes them a step further, so that our concern for others requires more of us than we originally thought:

> If you love those who love you, what credit is that to you? For even sinners love those who love them. If you do good to those who do good to you, what credit is that to you? For even sinners do the same. If you lend to those from whom you hope to receive, what credit is that to you? Even sinners lend to sinners, to receive as much again. But love your enemies, do good, and lend, expecting nothing in return. Your reward will be great, and you will be children of the Most High; for he is kind to the ungrateful and the wicked. (Luke 6:32-35)

Concern for the good of others is not confined to family and friends who are close to us nor even to those we admire and might consider worthy of our concern. We are not truly living a good life unless we care about the well-being of others indiscriminately, without regard for their worthiness. That, of course, vastly increases the number of claimants for whom we might have to set aside our own immediate good to attend to theirs.

Yet the risks in Jesus' teaching are not only that we might end up doing a lot more good for others than we bargained for. There is also the warning that we may find ourselves set in opposition to others at some cost to our own immediate good. Willingness to endure that kind of loss is not just facing up to an unpleasant possibility. It may be part of what it means to live a good life.

> Blessed are those who are persecuted for righteousness' sake, for theirs is the kingdom of heaven. Blessed are you when people revile you and persecute you and utter all kinds of evil against you falsely on my account. Rejoice and be glad, for your reward is great in heaven, for in the same way they persecuted the prophets who were before you. (Matt 5:10-12)[2]

Clearly, this business of living a good life is difficult! It can't be done simply by seeking what is obviously good for me. More than that, if the teachings of Jesus tell us anything about what makes a life good, it sometimes involves putting others' good ahead of our own. But caring about the good life of other people is not a simple matter of helping them get what they say they want. It may involve standing for truths that will arouse their hostility and misunderstanding, so that my safety is jeopardized and their peace is disturbed.

Living a Christian life sometimes leads us so far away from what we first think of as a good life that some Christians have argued that seeking a good life and living the Christian life are two very different things.

Seeking a good life is a self-centered effort, they say, and even if we sometimes manage to expand the circle of self-concern to include a few other people whose welfare is closely bound up with ours, we are still at the center. In the Christian life, by contrast, God is at the center, and questions about my own good become irrelevant. Augustine (354–430 CE) imagined humanity divided between two allegiances, one to an earthly or human city and the other to the City of God. The choice between them is absolute, and there can be no middle ground: "We see then that the two cities were created by two kinds of love: the earthly city was created by self-love reaching the point of contempt for God, the Heavenly City by the love of God carried as far as contempt of self."[3]

From this point of view, the delicate balance between the self and others and the tension between obedience to God and concern for self are swallowed up in one great determination that makes you a citizen either of the City of God or of the human city. After that, self-concern is either all-controlling or it counts for nothing.

From this point of view, too, ethics clearly belongs to the human city. Ethics, at least as Aristotle understood it, as the study of the good life for human beings, has no place in the city where everything is centered on the love of God.

To make that the last word, however, forgets that alongside the Christian's love for God, there is the biblical witness that God loves us. Jesus says that the purpose of his coming is freedom and abundant life (John 8:32; 10:10). The Bible as a whole bears witness to the goodness of creation (Gen 1:31) and its fitness for our habitation (Isa 45:18). Love for God is lived out in a world that is suited to human purposes.

Understanding in these biblical terms the world in which our life is lived gives us a way to think about our good that makes it more than something we have to set aside to serve others or something that we have to give up in order to love God. If this is a world created by God as a place for human life, then our search for a good life, difficult and confusing as it may sometimes be, is not something that we have to give up in order to be a part of God's people. But we do have to pursue the good life in the context of a world that is shaped by God's love for us. Belief in God as the creator of a good world is less a narrative of how the world came into being than it is a fundamental confidence that we can live our lives in harmony with the natural world around us rather than in vigilant resistance to its forces or determined efforts to subdue it by technology. The search for a good life is not a struggle to wrest peace and happiness from a hostile or indifferent universe. Belief that God has created us for life in this world suggests also that human good is not achieved by resistance to the claims of others, but by a common life in which we may achieve a greater good together than any of us controls alone.

Because the world is this way, living as though you could achieve a good life all by yourself, wresting control of things and events from other people and never asking any questions except "What do I want?" and "How can I get it?" is the greatest mistake of all. Though we may envy those who appear to live their lives on these terms and may sometimes try to act like them, the project is always less successful that it appears to be. Coworkers may quickly rise to the top by relentless self-promotion, but when we try it, the continuous tooting of our own horn turns out to be even more boring than listening to the sound of theirs. Celebrities may seem to enjoy gratifying their impulses for an appreciative media audience, but we find that even when we have the means to do exactly what we want, it is hard to know exactly what that is when we have no one to consult about it but ourselves. Attempts to achieve a good life by asking "What is good for me?" and then going out to get it are self-defeating. We may achieve our goal, but it will not be what we really wanted.

The inevitable failure of self-centered pursuits may drive us to the opposite extreme of despising ourselves, but that is not the real alternative. The real alternative is to live in harmony with nature and with other people, understanding that the limits they set on our self-chosen pursuits are not obstacles to a good life, but the framework on which it can be built. Acknowledging that we are not the center of the universe is not a choice against our good, but a recognition of what our good truly is.

To be sure, once we recognize this we will do many things that the purely self-centered person would never do. We give up vacations to put new roofs on houses for the rural poor or spend free afternoons in court with troubled adolescents. We live more modestly than our income would allow in order to give more to help people we most likely will never meet. We devote ourselves to projects whose conclusion we will never see, and we tie our happiness to the success of ventures that are not under our control. The successes will be limited, and perhaps they will become even more limited as our aspirations grow larger.

There are risks to all of this. Not everyone will cooperate with these efforts toward mutual improvement. Some will resent our efforts to help them, and we will resent some of the demands that others make on us. Occasionally, people will appropriate the results of our labors for their own purposes. And sometimes this diffuse mixture of risks will crystallize into what appears to be a genuine defeat: A stray bullet ends the life of a teacher who has devoted himself to stopping gang violence, or a doctor succumbs to a disease she contracted because she volunteered to treat it in others. There are no guarantees of temporal success when we seek a good life in harmony with nature and with other people. We may be defeated by circumstances or by the opposition of others. But even that is a better life than being defeated by ourselves.

So the Christian life, like the good life, is in one sense entirely natural. The Christian life is not a choice against the good life that other people obviously seek for themselves. The Christian life is this search for the good life in a world created by God. God's creation sets natural limits on our lives and sets us in relationships with other people, and our good must be found within those limits and relationships. But because the world is God's creation, we trust that our good is not in conflict with the fundamental conditions of our life. We will often be required to do things that run counter to our immediate wishes, and we may sometimes have to sacrifice a great deal. But the good life is not an accident that we fall into when nothing bad happens to us, nor is it a prize we must win by pushing aside other people and nature when they get in our way.

Choices

But the most difficult part of living a good life is not that we have to do things that we do not immediately want to do. We can understand that. What troubles us is that sometimes we do not even know what to do. We want to live in harmony with our children, especially as they and we grow older. That seems to be basic to a good life. But how do we secure that result? Will punishment now help them to acquire the self-discipline they need to become secure and responsible adults, or will it turn them into angry and resentful misfits? A compassionate response to people in need seems more appropriate to the good life than a scowling, suspicious attitude that presumes that the poor are mostly responsible for their own problems. But what attitude should I take toward people who really are irresponsible? Violence surely cannot be part of a good life. But what do I do about violent and aggressive people who threaten my good and that of people around me? Should I fight force with force, taking up the violence that my search for the good has rejected? Or do I withdraw and leave it to others to sacrifice their good lives to restrain the aggressor?

If the good life is natural, then why doesn't it come to us naturally, the way it comes to birds and bees and oak trees? Or even the way it comes to our cats and dogs? They are easily contented, and though they are sometimes momentarily confused or temporarily frustrated, they do not appear to have difficulty deciding what they want. Why is our search for a good life different?

To answer that question we have to go back to Aristotle, who noted that though all things pursue their good by nature, human beings alone fulfill this requirement of their nature by *deliberation*. That is, humans pursue their good not automatically or by instinct, but by thinking about what they might do and choosing the course that seems to lead to a good life. Humans pursue the good by using their reason to weigh their desires against one another, to determine the best means to achieve their goals and to secure those achievements for the future. This kind of thinking Aristotle called "practical reason," to distinguish it from the theoretical reason we use to develop our ideas about the world. Theoretical reason formulates what we know. Practical reason makes choices about what we are to do.

Choice, then, is how we shape a good life. Living in harmony with nature and with other people is not a matter of just doing what comes naturally. It requires us to think about our choices, drawing on what we know about the world and what we have learned in our own experience, not so much to test the truth of what we think as to determine what we are going to do. Each choice involves deciding what the good is for us in that situation. And the sum of all our choices becomes a statement, more powerful and fundamentally more honest than anything we might write down on paper, about what we believe the good life is.

Ethics

Ethics is the study of our choices about the good life, both individually and in the whole picture of a good life that our choices, taken together, create. Ethics is about the terribly difficult choices we face one at a time—whether to terminate the medical procedures that are keeping an elderly relative alive, whether to stand up and object when everyone around us seems to be accepting a dishonest policy, whether to give up the security of a boring job for a risky challenge that motivates us, whether to open our lives to people who may be very different from ourselves or to keep our distance by following patterns of judgment that we learned a long time ago. But ethics is also about how we understand the results of all our choices—who we are as a result of what we have done and what we decided not to do, what we have given to others over the course of our lives and what we have made of the things we have kept for ourselves.

We will be following some of those questions in detail in the chapters ahead. Before we begin, however, it is important to explain some key terms in order to understand how we will be using them and to clarify the point of view from which *Christian Ethics: An Essential Guide* is written.

Ethics, the study of the choices by which we try to live a good life, is sometimes distinguished from *morals*, the practices and beliefs by which people live. Ethics, then, is about thoughtful, reflective, and self-conscious decisions. Morals are the rules people follow without thinking about them. This can be a useful distinction, though with the diversity of religions and beliefs in contemporary society and the rapid changes in the ways our lives are lived, people have fewer opportunities than perhaps they once did to simply follow the rules without thinking about their choices. If we are going to make a distinction between an ethical choice and a moral choice, then the circumstances of our lives would appear to be forcing us to make more and more ethical choices.

However, it is easy to overstate the difference between ethics and morals. In fact, the difference between the English words *ethics* and *morals* derives from their origin in Greek (*ethos*) and Latin (*mores*), respectively. In the original languages both words mean the same thing—that is, the shared beliefs and practices of a people. In this book, we will use "ethics" and "morals" more or less as synonyms. Likewise, for present purposes, the adjectives "ethical" and "moral" will be largely interchangeable.

There is, however, another use of "moral" that should be noted. Moral goods, such as justice, honesty, or compassion, are sometimes distinguished from natural or nonmoral goods, such as health, wealth, comfort, and security, which are things that people want for themselves. (To say that a good is "nonmoral," of course, is very different from saying that it is "immoral.") A distinction between moral and nonmoral goods supposes that there is a real difference between the requirements of living a moral life and the things that we would seek as part of a (naturally or nonmorally) good life. In this book, as I have suggested already, we will follow a more Aristotelian understanding that sees moral goods as essential to a good life in the full sense, so that honesty and compassion are as much a part of the good life as comfort or security is. Thus you will not find here the sharp distinction between moral goods and nonmoral goods that some writers make, although I will sometimes refer to "the moral life," rather than to "the good life" when our discussion focuses more on the ways that our choices are shaped by our relations to other people and their needs than by our more immediate wants and wishes.

While we are paying attention to distinctions, let me mention another one that is often made. People might ask whether this book is an introduction to ethics, or an introduction to *Christian* ethics. The issue here is more than merely terminological. It has to do with how you understand the relationship between the good life and the Christian life. For some Christians, as we have seen, the choice between love of God and love of self is so absolute that you really cannot love God and at the same time care about your own good life. This does not mean that Christians have to live wretched, miserable lives. It just means that worrying about whether their lives are good lives or not is not on the Christians' agenda.

Some nonreligious writers stress a similar distinction. The Christian, the Jew, and the Muslim are each trying to make choices about life with a view to pleasing God and doing what God commands, while the moral life is about doing what is good for its own sake and making our own decisions about it. Worrying about whether one's life is pleasing to God just is not on the ethical agenda.

Understood in these ways, ethics and the Christian faith are asking quite different questions about life. Christian ethics would be thinking about how to live life in Christian terms, and ethics would be about how to make choices about life without considering a relationship to God or the teachings of a particular religious tradition. From this point of view, this book would have to be an introduction to Christian ethics.

The perspective in this book, it should already be clear, is quite different. There are resources for thinking about ethics in the Bible and in Christian tradition that are not so influential in other religions or traditions. Because Christians use these distinctive resources, it is likely that their first answers to questions about ethics will vary from those given by persons in other traditions; and some of these differences may persist even after extended discussions. There will be times when Christians will want to step back from the specifics of their faith and tradition to discuss what agreements they can come to about how to live together in community with all their neighbors, including those of other faiths and of no faith. Not all the ethics that Christians do has to be specifically Christian ethics. The shared questions about how to live a good life give us a great deal to occupy our attention together, even when we differ on important questions about whether there is a God and how we should relate to God. Christians and non-Christians probably will offer different answers in ethics, but they are asking the same questions. So this book is an introduction to some of the key questions of ethics, with special attention to the way Christians answer those questions. Just as we will speak of "the moral life" and "the good life," understanding that the two cannot be sharply separated, we will speak about "the Christian moral life" without implying that it is about something fundamentally different from the moral concerns that many other people also share.

One final note about terminology: Like several other words we have inherited from the Greeks, including *physics* and *mathematics*, the word *ethics* in modern English is a singular noun that ends in "s." So the right way to use it is to say, "Ethics *is* the study of our decisions about the good life," not "Ethics *are* the ways that people think about their choices." The earlier, obsolete usage of the word *ethic* as the singular is sometimes used to speak of "a Christian ethic," for example, or "a Buddhist ethic," as if each community had its own and all of them collectively make up "ethics." In general use, however, "a Christian ethics" is correct, and if you want more than one of them, you have to resort to something like "systems of Christian ethics."

How to Use This Book

So ethics is about important and difficult questions that are deeply rooted in Christian thinking and widely shared by people who are trying to live a good life in today's perplexing world. But ethics is not a simple list of the right answers to these questions. Those who turn to *Christian Ethics: An Essential Guide* hoping to find a paragraph that would give the Christian answer on assisted suicide, abortion, homosexuality, war, or welfare will not find what they are seeking. That is not just because controversial questions that have been widely studied and debated in recent years require more space than we can give them here. It is also because living a good life requires making choices for yourself, not learning someone else's answers.

It is possible to study the ethics of a community. We can find out whether people believe that abortion is right or wrong and what reasons they are likely to give for their answers. But that sort of *descriptive* ethics does not make our choices for us, even if the community whose answers and reasons are being studied is our own. Descriptive ethics is an important field of study, but when we are asking our own moral questions, they are questions of *normative* ethics. We want to know how to choose and how to think about choosing in ways that will help us make good decisions. If all we want to know is what other people have chosen, we are not really making a moral choice at all.

Real choices are complex and often very difficult. We also keep stumbling over new questions all the time, so that just when we think we have a set of moral answers that works pretty well for us, someone creates a new technology that gives us a new set of possibilities or we find ourselves in a new situation that we had not thought about before.

Fortunately, the ways of thinking about moral questions are not as numerous as the questions themselves. There are, in fact, just three main ways of thinking in ethics. When we have to make a choice, we can ask ourselves what goal we are seeking. We can try to decide whether a goal that is before us has a place in the good life and ask ourselves whether the course of action we are thinking about will, in fact, help us to achieve that goal. For a second way of thinking, we can also ask whether there are rules that we should follow when we are trying to make this sort of choice. Deciding what we ought to do cannot be reduced to figuring out what we want—difficult as that may be. We also think about whether there are some things that we should not do while we are reaching for our goals or some things that we ought to do when we have a chance, whether or not they get us closer to what we want. Finally, we can ask about something that is neither a rule nor a result, at least not in the way we usually think of results. We can ask what sort of person am I likely to become if I make this choice and keep making others like it. What would my character be like and what sort of virtues and vices would I have if I let choices like this one become a habit?

Those, broadly speaking, are the three ways to guide our thinking about moral choices: goals, rules, and virtues. It is possible to find answers to moral questions that other people have given, and sometimes that helps us sort out our questions. But if we want to answer the questions for ourselves, we will think about the goals, rules, and virtues that apply to these choices. That is when we are doing ethics. And the study of ethics is not so much a matter of learning answers that other people have arrived at as it is learning what we need to know about goals, rules, and virtues in order to be prepared to answer our moral questions.

Ethical specialists, of course, will produce theories that explain the relationships between goals, rules, and virtues. The theories tend to establish one sort of guide or another as primary. *Teleological* theories make our moral choices dependent on goals, so that our rules and virtues help us achieve our goals. *Deontological* theories put the stress on rules, so that we choose our goals within the limits set by rules and seek those virtues that make us better at following the rules. Theories of virtue, which are sometimes called *areteological* theories, suggest that what we do and what we choose is in the end less significant than the kind of people we become.

We will learn something about these types of ethical theory in the course of this book, but our primary interest is not in deciding between the theories, just as it is not in learning about the answers that others have given to important moral questions. Our purpose in this brief intro-duction to ethics is reflection on the Christian moral life, on how we make our choices as Christians who are seeking to live a good life. Most of us find that we need goals, rules, and virtues in order to guide those choices.

So that is where we will turn in the next three chapters. We will look at how goals, rules, and virtues figure in the choices that everyone makes in the search for a good life. And we will give special consideration to what Christian Scripture says about these things and what writers and teach-ers throughout Christian history have thought about them. Then we will turn to two chapters that discuss how we make these choices in the church and in society and to a brief conclusion that returns to the ques-tion of how our search for the good life relates to our faith in God.

CHAPTER 2

Goals

Although we spend much of our time seeking a good life, we do not often think about the good life in general. Our attention is focused on more specific goals, and that is how our lives are shaped and measured. We have so many decisions to make that we could not decide at all without some idea about where we want those choices to take us. There are so many things that we could do and so few that we can actually get done that we wander from impulse to impulse unless we have a goal in mind.

This emphasis on goals is most apparent in our work lives. Businesses of every sort develop strategic plans to set goals for their operations and place themselves in relation to their competitors. Managers try to define goals that are measurable and achievable, and they try to communicate these goals to every part of the business, so that the goals become part of everyone's work.

This goal setting and goal seeking that is essential to a profit-making business has also become an expectation in nonprofit organizations, so that schools, hospitals, and service agencies also formulate mission statements and try to communicate their goals to volunteers and employees and to a wider community of supporters. Even churches engage their members in determining priorities and setting goals that can be measured and achieved.

It sounds appropriate when people tell us that their church is working on a mission statement, but it usually turns out that the project owes more to management theory than to mission in the traditional ecclesiastical sense. The point of the mission statement, for a congregation no less than for a corporation, is to formulate its purposes in ways that will allow it to be specific and selective about its goals. So every group to which we belong, from the place where we work to the place where we worship, urges us to keep our goals before us, to shape our choices and actions in the present around the places we want to be and think we can be in the future.

When we come closer to home, to the lives we share with our families and the personal space we create for ourselves, the goal-setting process is usually less explicit. The goals we set for our lives as a whole may not be so easy to measure, and the strategic plan for achieving those goals is less definite. Even the goals themselves may be less articulate. Our personal goals may be so intimate that we rarely speak about them or so basic to our lives that we no longer have to think very much about them. In the worst case, our personal goals may be so buried under the mass of goals that other people have set for us that we no longer know what our own goals are.

But the goals are there, nonetheless. They give shape to our lives, and over time they make us who we are. Our goals provide the clearest picture of what we think belongs in that good life everyone is seeking. Our goals say what we think is really valuable, what is worth wanting. Through our goals we tell ourselves and others what choices we think we ought to make in order to achieve the good life. So our goals are an indispensable part of our ethics.

But that is not how we usually think about ethics. Ethics is supposed to be about hard choices, like what to do when you have seven people in a lifeboat built to hold six. Ethics is supposed to be about rules, like do not cheat on your income tax and do not take credit for work you did not do. Rules tell us what to do, but they do not necessarily help us decide what we want. So we have a hard time seeing the link between our goals and ethics.

We have a similar problem connecting goals to our faith. Faith, in fact, may seem most relevant when our goals have failed us. We turn to faith when our hopes are disappointed and we are uncertain about the future, and we are surely right to do so. There is comfort and courage in the promise that God is with us, no matter what happens. We pray, "Thy will be done," at points when it is clear that God's will is different from what we want.

Often we are less clear about how God's will might be done through the goals that we set for ourselves. We reserve our faith for the truly important choices that may never come, and we turn instead to advice columns in the newspaper. We buy self-help books at the bookstore, and we eagerly anticipate the next issue of our favorite lifestyle magazine. People are always looking for advice on how to set goals and achieve them. If they mostly doze through sermons and skip the ethics seminars at work, perhaps they do so because they have not yet seen the connection between goals and ethics or between goals and faith. Goals are central to our life today. We cannot expect any faith or ethics to speak to us if it does not speak to our goals.

Goals and Goods

Ethicists call the object of a goal a "good." A good is a specific thing we are seeking when we set a goal. Wealth, career success, or a secure home life are all goods in this sense. (The way economists refer to products as "goods" is derived from this use in ethics. The "goods and services" that economists measure are the goals of productive processes that businesses undertake.) A system of ethics that gives primary attention to the goals or goods that we achieve by our actions is called a *teleology* or a *teleological ethics*.[1]

Teleological ethics reached its fullest development in Britain and North America toward the end of the 1700s when politicians and philosophers were trying to build democracy and create new, modern institutions for education, government, and business life. It seemed to some of them that the key task of ethics was to identify a single good that could encompass all of our goals. We could simplify morality if we could just substitute one clearly stated goal for all the complexities of law and all the rigidities of morality that had grown up during the previous centuries. Adam Smith (1723–90), the founder of the modern study of economics, began his career as a moral philosopher. He urged people to adopt free markets in part because he thought they were more efficient ways to make choices than rules and traditions could prescribe.

Jeremy Bentham (1748–1832) and John Stuart Mill (1806–73) proposed a system of ethics that became known as *utilitarianism*. Utilitarianism is based on the simple principle that we should always do the thing that "results in the greatest happiness of all those whose interest is in question." This principle, Bentham asserted, is the best guide "not only of every action of a private individual, but of every measure of government."[2] At a time of rapid social change, when it seemed to many people that morality was little more than age-old custom or superstition, the utilitarians' emphasis on the goal rather than on the rules seemed to offer clearer answers that made sense to the people who had to live by them.

In the history of ethics an emphasis on goods or goals often reappears when the accepted rules seem no longer to provide answers to the moral questions people really have. At the end of the nineteenth century, Rev. C. M. Sheldon wrote the classic novel *In His Steps* in an effort to show that the difficult new problems of life in an urban, industrial society could be solved by asking at every point where we have to make a choice about action, "What would Jesus do?"[3] In the 1960s as people struggled with new patterns in family life, new possibilities in medicine, and the political problems of welfare, race, and poverty, *situation ethics* promised that the answers would become clear if we simply made love the one rule in every situation where we face a choice.[4] Like utilitarianism, which tells us that the moral choice is the one that maximizes happiness for all concerned, situation ethics or *agapism* (from the Greek word for love, *agape*) tries to cut through the maze of conflicting rules, out-of-date advice, and burdensome regulations by suggesting a single goal against which all of our choices can be measured.

The simplicity of these prescriptions is appealing, but it quickly becomes apparent that it is difficult to find the single goal against which all of our choices could be measured. The utilitarian tells us to create the greatest happiness for all, but how do I compare your happiness and mine? Who is happier, the opera fan when the curtain comes down at the end of *Lohengrin* or the soap opera fan at the end of another episode of "Days of Our Lives"? The naturalist hiking through an unspoiled forest or a timber worker returning home at the end of a hard day of logging?

Moral systems that maximize some one good, such as utilitarianism (happiness) or agapism (love) work well only when we can measure all the different goods that people seek against a single standard. In a democratic society we can give everyone a vote and decide what creates the most happiness by seeing which goal gets the most votes. In a market economy dollars or yen or euros provide the measure. People determine what creates the most happiness in a rough and ready way by deciding what they will buy and how much they will pay for it or by what they expect to be paid for something that provides happiness to another person.

Such economic measures provide an efficient way to decide how much a product or service is worth, but we do not have to think about it very long to realize that these utilitiarian systems do not tell us what we really want to know about our moral life. Market economics is no substitute for ethics. The problem is not just that we have a hard time finding a goal that will measure competing goods among different people. We have a hard time finding one goal that will cover all of the things we think belong in our own good life.

The Diversity of Goods

We may try to find some one goal, whether it is happiness, or love, or cold, hard cash; but we quickly find that the goods we pursue are irreducibly multiple. We just cannot say how much the happiness that comes from doing a good job is worth compared with the happiness that comes from spending an evening at home with the family or volunteering at a tutoring center. We cannot compare the satisfaction of playing the cello, even though it is done poorly, with the satisfaction of being a really good real estate salesperson or a Little League coach with a winning season. Our goals are different, and the moral task, whether it is between ourselves and other persons or just within our individual lives, is to strike a balance between these irreducibly different goals, to find some way of putting them together that enables us to live good lives individually and together.

This task is more difficult than coming up with a list of goods we want—such as job security, opportunity to travel, a comfortable home—or coming up with a list of goods that we think everyone in society should be entitled to have—an opportunity to work, health care, protection against exploitation, for example. We have to find a combination of goals that work together to make a complete life for the individual who pursues them. The goods that individuals seek must also allow for cooperation with others, or competition for scarce resources will result in anxiety and insecurity for everyone. At least some of our goals must be shared. And the goods that all of us seek must be sustainable. They must be goals that not only offer us a reasonable chance of success in attaining them, but also such that our success will not prevent generations who come after us from enjoying those goods too.

The list of goods that are of general concern will include some that the philosophers call "basic goods," meaning that they are essential to almost every idea of a good life that we can imagine. We have to have food, clothing, and shelter. We have to have medical care when we are ill and help when we are injured or incapacitated. We need to have enough of these basic goods so that our time is not spent entirely on finding shelter for the night or a meal for the day. We not only need these basic goods today; we need to feel secure about them for the future. We need assurance that bad luck or bad choices will not leave our lives irretrievably broken.

Basic goods are not simply material necessities. Freedom to make our own choices and hold to our own beliefs is also a basic good. We would not think we had achieved the good life if the price we had to pay for material security was the surrender of control over our future or the denial of beliefs and values we hold most dear. Likewise, we cannot imagine a good life, no matter how prosperous and secure, without the basic good of self-respect. We have to be able to say, "I am somebody," and believe it, in order to live a good life. In most cases that means we need both a community that supports us and cares for us and signs of respect from the wider society, so that even strangers treat us as if we are somebody.

We cannot neglect these basic goods when setting goals for our lives. Indeed, when we think about goals politically, much of the discussion is about how to ensure that everyone has access to these basic goods, what kinds of respect to enforce by law and what kinds of care to require from parents, families, and others. When we think about the basic goods that everyone needs, the questions often concern how to divide responsibility for obtaining them between individuals and the community.

Yet even in regard to basic goods, individuals have to make choices for themselves. For some people, having a good life is closely related to a secure supply of these basic goods and especially to knowing that their families are secure. Others are ready to accept less of the basic goods in order to have an opportunity for new experiences or to acquire an education or to set up a business that offers them greater prospects for long-term satisfaction, even if these opportunities also pose greater risks. For some, security is what the good life is all about. For others, security is stifling and limiting.

It is at this point, as we move beyond the basic goods that everyone has to have in order to pursue any other goals, that we come the goals that are most clearly our own, and to the most personal part of ethics. To say that this is personal does not mean that we can choose whatever goals we like or that we cannot be held accountable for the choices. But it does mean that if the choices are to be *moral* choices, they must be truly our own. We cannot simply let others choose for us. Nor can we suppose that there is a universal ordering of goods and goals that makes all the choices for us, as though it were always better to choose grand opera rather than soap opera or always right to place family above work.

The task of ethics is neither to rank possible goals in some sort of order nor to find some one goal in terms of which all the rest can be measured. The task is to find a combination of goals that can guide us in living a good life. Because these goals are irreducibly different and often cannot be measured against one another, there is no easy, objective rule that will tell us when we have done this right. Our goals change throughout our lives, and the mix that each person seeks will be distinctive and different from the goals of any other person. Yet we do not set our goals randomly or without reflection. And we do not set them alone. Others may assist us in the choices when we find them difficult or hold us accountable when we have made them too easy for ourselves. Perhaps most important, the choices that others have made help us to see what is possible for ourselves. In light of their goals we see more clearly what we want—and what we want to avoid.

Ways of Life

Students of ethics today pay far more attention to the variety and diversity of goals than they did in the past. The Greek philosophers who first set the terms for the study of ethics assumed that the only people with moral choices to make were free, adult, male citizens who had the leisure and opportunity for discussion, for participation in politics, and for the pursuit of civic and military honors. Other people were constrained by the need to devote themselves to household activities or had their goals chosen for them by their superiors or were unable to live good lives because they lacked the requisite physical or mental abilities.

For Aristotle, those who were fortunate enough to make choices about their lives had two basic options. They could pursue the goals that make up an "active" life: the effort to win recognition, public office, and authority in the city. Or they could adopt the "contemplative" life: seeking knowledge and understanding and avoiding the turmoil and anxiety that go with participation in public affairs. Debate among Aristotle's followers revolved around which of these lives was better and whether it was possible in some way to combine the goals of action and contemplation in a "mixed" way of life, engaged with the struggles of the moment and yet lifted above them by a wider understanding of the enduring realities.[5]

Much later, Christian writers like Augustine (354–430 CE) dealt with this same tension between the active role of leadership in society and in the church and a life of contemplation lived in a monastic community. In the waning days of the Roman Empire, Augustine attempted to combine the choices. He took an increasingly active role as a public authority in the North African province where he lived, and he encouraged wealthy and highly placed Christian citizens to serve as judges, city administrators, and the like. But he also insisted that the true human good could not be found in a political community, whose goals were confined to this world; and he organized his clergy into a monastic community that lived by a strict rule that centered on prayer and on disciplined withdrawal from the pains and pleasures of secular life.

By the end of the Middle Ages, the superiority of the contemplative life was well established in principle, although the attractions of secular power were such that the eldest sons who inherited that power first usually left the contemplative life to their younger brothers or to their sisters. In any case, the range of choices was limited, and the number of those who had any real opportunity to choose was small.

Early in the 1500s the Protestant Reformation and the beginnings of modern forms of government and business led to a rethinking of the relationship between religious life and other ways of living. All Christians, Martin Luther (1483–1546) insisted, share in the priesthood, serving one another as ministers of God's grace. Those who labor for the benefit of their neighbors in even the most humble occupations have a vocation or calling (*vocatio*) as important as the religious vocations of monks and nuns.

In practice this modern expansion of the concept of Christian vocation did not reach very many people, even in highly developed industrialized countries, until the twentieth century. Most people had few possibilities for education and little freedom to seek new opportunities. Women were often excluded from roles that took them beyond home and family. Persons with physical limitations, mental illnesses, or other conditions that distinguished them from the majority of the population could be restricted, excluded from everyday life, and discouraged from fully developing the capacities they had.

Many people continue to suffer from the lack of these basic goods, and the challenge of providing those goods in a just and sustainable way for all the world's people is perhaps the most difficult moral problem we face as a world community on the edge of the twenty-first century. However, for the relatively well-off citizens of highly developed nations in North America and Europe—a group that includes most readers of books like this one—the proliferation of choices in personal goals during the twentieth century has made for dramatic changes in ethics. We are no longer constrained by the same kinds of scarcity in basic goods that our ancestors faced. Our material needs are more adequately met, and the spread of democratic political systems offers us more freedom and opportunity. We have more kinds of work available to us, and our work no longer determines our lives as it did when hours were longer and labor was more intensely physical. Physical or mental challenges need no longer confine us to the margins of life or to sheltered dependency in the ways they once did. We are less tied to domestic roles that subordinate goals and talents to the needs of spouses and children, and more free to pursue our interests as individuals.

The result is an array of new choices that has not always been matched by fresh thinking about our moral lives. Neither an old-fashioned moralism that equates morality with nineteenth-century patterns of work and family life nor a modern individualism that insists we are free to do anything we like (as long as we do not harm anyone else, of course) will provide the guidance we need.

Directions begin to become clearer, however, if we remember that our goals give direction to our choices primarily by identifying the personal qualities and skills that we need to develop in order to achieve the goals. To be sure, we may state our goals in terms of things we want to have or do—"My goal is to earn a degree and get a promotion," or "My goal is to see the great museums of Europe"—but those goals are shorthand for the things we will have to do to prepare for the goal and the kind of personal qualities we will need to cultivate in order to appreciate the goal when we achieve it. It is easy to become confused at this point, because a lot of products and services are sold by turning this thinking around.

"When I acquire this automobile," we are supposed to think, "I will be the kind of person I want to be because that is the kind of person who is driving this automobile in the commercial." "When I have seen the great museums of Europe, I will be the kind of person who understands and appreciates art because that is the kind of person who signs up for the tour to see those museums."

Thinking about our goals in terms of skills and personal qualities that we want to develop focuses our thinking because it makes it more clear what we will have to do now in order to achieve the goal and makes it evident at the outset that there are some prerequisites that have to be met if it is going to make any sense at all for me to have this goal. I may say, quite confidently, on the Fourth of July that my goal is to do something special for the homeless next Christmas season; but if that is a goal, and not just a wish or a fantasy, then I should be inquiring now about organizations that need volunteers for community service in the fall or talking to pastors and volunteers and social workers who worked with the homeless last Christmas to find out what the greatest problems were and what needs went unmet.

In short, I need to be working today on the knowledge and skills I will need to meet my goal, even if the goal is months or years in the future. And of course, if I already know that my job is going to take me to Bahrain next December, then this probably is not a goal I can have at all. Similarly, I can always have a goal of improving my personal fitness or my performance in some amateur athletic contest; but if I do not begin with a relatively high level strength, speed, and coordination, being an Olympic competitor probably is not a goal for me. For many of the goals that I might make a part of a good life, I have to be in a position to make certain commitments, and I need the capacity to acquire certain skills before I can really choose that goal for myself.

Because people differ so much in their interests and abilities, studies in ethics have often treated these choices as if they were not primarily moral questions. There seems to be no one answer that can be required. Yet precisely because the options before us here are so wide, these are the choices that are sometimes most deeply troubling to conscientious individuals. How can I act responsibly in choosing which talents to develop and which commitments to make? Does it matter morally what I choose? Or is this a situation in which the only right choice is the one that is right for me?

Stewardship and Community

In contrast to the individualism that thinks of these choices as too personal for moral evaluation, Christian ethics says that it makes a difference what we do with the powers and opportunities that are most distinctly our own. From a very early point Christian writers have treated these things neither as lucky accidents to be used for personal advantage nor as private possessions that can be disposed of however their holders wish. The appropriate way to regard one's abilities and opportunities, as Paul argues in Romans, is to see them as gifts:

> For as in one body we have many members, and not all the members have the same function, so we, who are many, are one body in Christ, and individually we are members one of another. We have gifts that differ according to the grace given to us: prophecy, in proportion to faith; ministry, in ministering; the teacher, in teaching; the exhorter, in exhortation; the giver, in generosity; the leader, in diligence; the compassionate, in cheerfulness. (Rom 12:4-8)

The variety of possibilities bestowed on us by our circumstances (the giver), our abilities (the exhorter), our place in the community (the leader), and our temperament (the compassionate) are to be understood in their diversity as gifts to be used and shared. The point is not to speculate about why some apparently have more gifts than others or about why I have this gift and not that one. The moral evaluation turns on how the gift is used.

In Paul's letters this is practical advice about the diversity of spiritual gifts within the Christian community, but the point seems to apply more generally. Jesus tells a parable about a group of servants who are entrusted with different amounts of their master's goods and left in charge of them for an extended period of time. When the master returns he rewards the servants who have used the time to increase his wealth and punishes the one who simply gave back what he had been given. The small amount he had to work with provides no excuse at the point of judgment. What matters is the use you make of what you have been given (Matt 25:14-30).

We must make our own choices about how we use our gifts, but those choices are subject to a wider judgment. In the New Testament two principles seem to govern that judgment.

The first is implicit already in the parable of the servants entrusted with their master's goods, and it is fundamental to Christian ethics. It is the principle of *stewardship*. What we have in the way of opportunities, abilities, resources, and so on are not simply ours to use up and discard. We are to care for these gifts and try to increase them. This has obvious relevance to the ways we use material goods and the ways we treat the environment, but it also applies to the abilities and powers we have as persons. In choosing our goals we should have an eye not just to the easiest and most immediate results, but to those achievements that will make

30

a larger and more lasting difference in our lives and in the lives of those around us.

Often this will mean developing talents that require long practice or rigorous education to bring out their full potential. Sometimes it will require us to focus rather narrowly on what we can do really well, in contrast to a wider and perhaps more comfortable range of competencies that we can develop to more ordinary levels. In any case, the principle of stewardship suggests that we should choose personal goals that require us to sharpen our capacities and make full use of our gifts rather than seeking out what comes easily to us. Living a good life may take many forms, but all of them involve working at real excellence in some selected areas of life where our gifts make that excellence possible.

The second principle is suggested by the way Paul speaks of individual gifts in the context of the whole church. It is the principle of *community*. Paul enjoins those who have spiritual gifts to think about how they can be used for the benefit of others. The aim is not simply high peaks of individual achievement, but a community in which the pursuit of our goals also enables others to live a good life. Minimally, the principle of community rules out selfish or exploitative goals, even when they require a high level of individual excellence. A person does not live a good life by developing the skills of manipulation and persuasion that allow one to prosper at the expense of others, and a community does not encourage excellence by arranging matters so that some people develop their skills as a result of keeping others in subordinate positions with limited possibilities.

Put more positively, the principle of community suggests that we should choose those goals that enrich the lives of other people and enable them to live good lives of their own. This requires thoughtful attention to the needs of others, but it also requires a careful assessment of our own needs so that we can develop the skills and capacities that will contribute most fully to the good of others. People who have the stamina, coordination, and intellect to be surgeons, or the patience and communicative skills to be teachers have possibilities to help many other people live good lives, but they will also have to seek support from many other people in order to achieve excellence in those endeavors.

The goals by which we build up the community are numerous, and it is not easy to say that one is better than another. When we think of gifts that can be developed to make a good life possible for others, we should not think only of surgeons and teachers. Entertainers can lift spirits and open imaginations. Accountants, computer specialists, and maintenance engineers can make many people's work smoother and more productive. A checkout clerk in the supermarket who is both efficient and friendly may contribute more to the good lives of people than a surly surgeon would. In the end, we must choose these personal and vocational goals for ourselves because there are just too many possibilities for anyone to say that there is just one way of life that is right. What we choose for ourselves, however, need not be chosen selfishly. Christian ethics suggests that we are most likely to achieve a good life by setting goals that develop our talents and make full use of our resources and by choosing which of our possibilities to develop, with a view to the impact these goals could have on the good lives of other people too.

Commitments

In a moral life guided by the principles of stewardship and community, choices become commitments. Our goals are so bound up with other people that a goal seriously chosen and acted upon is not easily undone. Every important choice makes commitments to others and connects my goals to theirs for the future, perhaps beyond the limits of my own life and actions.

Such goals both limit our choices and expand them. We are limited as we realize that the goals we can set in the future are limited not only by the gifts and resources we happen to have, but also by the commitments we have already made. The choice to marry, decisions about what to study and where to study it, moving to a specific community, or joining a particular congregation—all these choices determine what goals we will be able to set in the future, often in ways that we cannot predict when we initially make the choices. Yet each choice also expands what we may do in the future by involving other people in the goals we have set and extending the horizon of our goals beyond the limits of our immediate action and beyond the length of our own lives.

One way of thinking about ethics has always cautioned against setting goals that take you beyond the boundaries of your life and the outcomes you can control. Aristotle questions whether we can count anyone happy until that person is dead. While this sounds strange, the point is sensible enough: Our plans are so subject to disappointment, failure, and sudden reversals of fortune that even the most successful person today may end up miserable tomorrow.[6] The Stoic philosophers who were active around the time Christianity began to spread rapidly through the ancient world carried that note of warning further and made it a central guide to the moral life. The wise person, according to Stoic teaching, is someone who avoids suffering by not depending on events and persons that one cannot control. (This is why we sometimes say that a person who bears loss and pain without showing it is stoical.) Epictetus (60–138 CE) counseled his readers:

A person's master is someone who has power over what he wants or does not want, either to obtain it or take it away. Whoever wants to be free, therefore, let him not want or avoid anything that is up to others. Otherwise, he will necessarily be a slave.[7]

Our contemporary culture offers similar warnings. We may talk less about avoiding pain and loss, but we worry constantly about security. Security is identified with having a wide range of future choices, so that we might paraphrase Aristotle by saying, "Count no one happy until that person is retired on a comfortable pension." Even the most successful executive may be downsized, and the key to happiness, we are told, is to set financial goals that will allow you to be independent and active, whatever happens to your pension plan or to the Social Security system. We hear echoes of the Stoic advice to avoid reliance on others for your happiness and to set goals that remain firmly under your own control.

Early Christian writers respected the Stoics for their self-discipline and their high moral standards, but they understood that Christian faith takes a very different approach. Christian faith has a bias toward goals that bind us to others and commit us to projects larger than our own lives. In contrast to the Stoic claim that wise people will keep happiness under their own control, Jesus' parables focus on a future that lies in God's hands. The rich fool in Luke 12:13-21 sets the goal of building new barns and storing up goods sufficient for many years of enjoyment, only to die on the very night that his plans are complete. The Stoic would agree that this man was foolish because he failed to understand that neither the security of his possessions nor the length of his life was really under his control. Jesus' advice, however, is not to avoid things that are not under your control, but to recognize that the only enduring purposes belong to God:

Do not keep striving for what you are to eat and what you are to drink, and do not keep worrying. For it is the nations of the world that strive after all these things, and your Father knows that you need them. Instead, strive for his kingdom, and these things will be given to you as well. (Luke 12:29-31)

The paradox that runs through the Gospels is that what seems most within our control is actually the least secure. God's purposes are the only certainties, even though they seem to be not only beyond our power, but beyond hope. In John's Gospel, Jesus says:

Very truly, I tell you, unless a grain of wheat falls into the earth and dies, it remains just a single grain; but if it dies, it bears much fruit. Those who love their life lose it, and those who hate their life in this world will keep it for eternal life. (John 12:24-25)

It simply isn't possible to seek a really important and lasting goal without relinquishing control of your own satisfactions. Wanting something that extends beyond the limits of your life and power exposes you to the risk that you will "lose your life," metaphorically and perhaps even literally. The most obvious examples come from marriage and family life. The goals of a good marriage and the goals of good parenting are not always compatible with a steady, satisfying good life in which I achieve my goals with predictable regularity. But such intimate connections of life with life can occur in many other partnerships. Churches become extended families, especially in these times when family structures are more tenuous and distances often separate us from traditional family relationships. Even business relationships are not excluded, although we usually try to keep their goals more limited. Wherever the search for a good life is truly shared, relationships take us beyond our individual goods and goals; and we find ourselves committed to goals that are larger and more lasting than anything we can create for ourselves.

Covenants

Such goals require commitments that are different from the goals we set primarily for ourselves. Personal goals can be changed rather quickly, as we discover that cello lessons or pottery classes are not as fulfilling as we had thought. Jobs and career goals can change dramatically, as the accountant goes to seminary or the high school teacher becomes a painter. Of course, even these personal goals require the cooperation of others who provide us with opportunities, teach us the skills we need, or join with us in various short-term projects. But where our goals are primarily personal, we try to keep these relationships limited. They are *contracts*, implicit or explicit, in which we specify what we need from others in order to achieve our goals, what we are prepared to give them in exchange for their cooperation, and how long we expect the relationship to last. Living up to these agreements is important, but it is also important that their terms be clearly stated and that everyone understands that the relationship exists primarily to further the individual goals of the parties involved.

It is important to note the differences between these contracts that people make to assist one another in achieving their individual goals and another kind of commitment that happens when people share a goal that is more important than their individual goals. Not seeing those differences can lead to some of the most bitter interpersonal conflicts. When one spouse thinks of marriage as a personal commitment that helps him become the kind of person he wants to be for now and the other spouse sees it as a lifetime commitment to family that may require dramatic changes in the couples' personal goals, the stage is set for a contentious marriage or an angry divorce. Likewise, when the owner of a growing business in which she has invested her life's goals and energy demands similar commitments from subordinates who regard their jobs as contractual employment, misunderstandings and recriminations are bound to arise.

Shared commitments to goals that are more important than our personal goals create *covenants*. We enter into them knowing that they may demand some changes in our personal goals. Though we should not take on the obligations of a covenant relationship without serious reflection on what it will require, we also know that covenants are somewhat open-ended. We cannot specify their limits as easily as we can with contracts. They may demand more of us than we first expect; and if their goals are sufficiently large, they may well last a lifetime. Here, indeed, we must be willing to risk our lives in order to obtain the life that goes with commitment to the goal.

In our initial enthusiasm for a covenant goal, we may accept the sacrifices it imposes eagerly; but if we are realistic about our weaknesses, we also know that there will be times when we will want to minimize these demands or evade the covenant's requirements, if possible. We understand the scripture about losing our life in order to find it, but there is also a part of us that wants to believe in having our cake and eating it too. For that reason, covenant obligations must sometimes take the form of rules, at least for setting minimum expectations. When our commitments are called into question, the rules, rather than the goals, may become the center of attention in the covenant. We will have more to say about covenant rules and their role in the moral life in chapter 3.

For the moment, however, our focus is not the rules that define the boundaries of the Christian moral life, but the goals that set its aspirations. To be willing to lose your life in order to keep it for eternal life is not only a matter of preparing yourself for life in heaven after death. It means living this life in the conviction that God's rule of justice and peace and God's care for those who are vulnerable, in need, and undefended are the really important goals in living, whatever else contemporary people may value and however slim the hope for achieving these ultimate purposes may appear. The good news of Jesus Christ is that those who hold to these goals cannot be defeated, despite appearances that they are weak, poor, and continually at risk of destruction by forces that know how to make better use of power to serve their more limited goals (2 Cor 4:7-12; 6:1-10).

These goals become real for us in specific commitments to organizations, programs, and other people. We do not work for justice abstractly conceived. We write letters for a human rights organization or become advocates for refugees who need help with immigration regulations. We become part of a congregation that provides breakfast at a local shelter for the homeless, sends a medical mission team to Central America, and supports missionaries and relief workers in Russia and Eastern Europe. We seek out programs that will connect us with people whose needs are very different from our own and who would be kept on the margins of our lives by the rest of the organizations to which we belong.

Yet these goals, if we really understand them, are so large that they outlast our commitments to individual projects and organizations. Commitment to God's justice shapes our lives across the years, even though the specific problems, people, and organizations that demand our time and attention may change. Care for the poor and vulnerable is part of why we are loyal to a congregation of fellow Christians, but it also shapes our choice of the next congregation we join when our lives change and employment, family, or education takes us to a new place. We may reach our goals for career, family, and personal development; but we see all these successes (and the occasional failure) in light of larger goals that will probably never be reached. Yet these larger goals shape our choices and commitments at every stage of our lives and become part of who we are, so that we can no longer imagine successes or commitments that do not include these transcendent goals, which are achieved in hope, but are constantly attended by risk and failure.

The Christian idea of the good life, in contrast to the Stoic aim of self-control, includes these goals that involve risk, have a high potential for failure, and lead us into covenant commitments to others. That is the paradox of a good life that includes a willingness to lose one's life. Missionaries and aid workers are put at risk by political unrest or by the ambitions of local demagogues. Doctors risk infection to aid those who are most vulnerable to disease. Teachers put up with unsafe buildings and violent communities in order to teach those who most need the opportunities that come with education. They do not always succeed. They often sacrifice their personal goals and sometimes give their lives in the effort. But it is they, and not the successful person whose commitment extends no farther than his or her own plans, who provide us with the examples of what a good life is. They have had important goals, and the risks they ran were the measure of how important the goals really were. Those who settled for smaller, safer purposes missed the goals that finally endure. They made the foolish choice to settle for a life that ended with full barns, and they made no commitments beyond that (Luke 12:13-21).

Goals and Plans

To live a good life we must know what we would be willing to die for. But most of our choices will be about living, not dying. If tragic circumstances require the sacrifice of our well-being in the service of those goals that are larger than our own lives, we may pray for courage to accept that loss, rather than betray the commitments that have shaped who we are and that are most important to us. But a grim determination to demonstrate our readiness to sacrifice may actually render us less effective in living our commitments.

Knowing what we are prepared to die for should yield a joyful commitment to goals that are more permanent and less vulnerable than our needs and desires. That commitment is lived in daily attention to how the choices we make really serve our goals. The goals we have chosen have to become guides to the many different small decisions that really shape our daily lives. Until that happens, they are goals in only the most vague sense. Having a real goal also means having a plan.

When goals become plans, then we recognize again the irreducible diversity of goods that we noted at the beginning of this chapter. Sometimes we can work on more than one goal at once. We may be able to turn a volunteer project that gives us a chance to help in others in the community into a family activity that gives us important time with our children, for example. But more often than not, several different goals are in competition for our time and resources in the present. We have to choose not only which goals are important and which are not, but also which of the important goals will command our attention now and which will be postponed, perhaps indefinitely.

All of us are familiar with these dilemmas. We think about them all the time, whether with the focused intensity of deliberate choice or with the vague uneasiness that troubles us when we know that we are neglecting what is most important in order to fix something that is more insistent. What we do not always understand is that these are moral questions. We devour books on time management and take seminars on goal setting and strategic planning in hopes of finding a technique that will solve the problem, when in fact we are making choices about the good life. Stephen Covey, one of the leading contemporary exponents of goal-setting and planning skills, is surely correct when he suggests that these questions about efficiency and personal effectiveness inevitably become questions about values and moral principles.[8] The questions they raise cannot be answered by a better scheduling technique or evaded by giving our time and attention to whatever is most urgent at the moment. For most of us, these questions about how our goals become plans and how the plans we make become connected to our goals are among the most important moral questions we will ever have to face. Certainly they are the most persistent.

To some, however, it may seem inappropriate or even unfaithful to link plans and planning with the goals that are central to a Christian moral life. That may work well enough for the plans that are strictly my own, the personal goals and achievements that fill up everyday life. I have to plan learning my part for the chorus in which I want to sing or building the cabinets I want my family to enjoy. I have to plan how to finish my degree or build my retirement savings. But how can I plan for world peace or racial reconciliation? And aren't those supposed to be God's goals, anyway? What right do I have to act as though I could set them back or bring them forward?

Early in the twentieth century a more optimistic generation of Christian thinkers closely linked the kingdom of God to the achievement of progressive political and economic goals in the rapidly developing urban industrial societies of Europe and North America. This Social Gospel movement, led especially by the Baptist theologian Walter Rauschenbusch, predicted that in the twentieth century Christian commitments would fundamentally transform the moral conditions of life, just as science and technology had transformed its material conditions during the nineteenth century.[9]

Those hopes were quickly disappointed by World War I, and theologians since about 1920 have placed more emphasis on the difference between God's will and our plans than on the connections between them. We are told by the theologians that political plans and social reforms "in themselves . . . are of no value. In no sense can they ever be even a first step towards the Kingdom of Heaven."[10] If we are attentive to our Christian experience, we learn, too, that our lives are changed most profoundly and our faith grows most rapidly at those points where God interrupts our plans with challenges we did not expect.

Faith does require a distance between my plans and God's purposes. My plans would be unfaithful if doing what I plan on behalf of justice and peace became so closely tied to justice and peace in my mind that I could not tolerate any other ways of working toward the goal. We see this happen with tragic results in politics when leaders conclude that they have been chosen to change history, therefore, that no further dissent or questions can be allowed. The mistake, however, is not made only by megalomaniac dictators. We also experience this in our offices, schools, and families. There it is sometimes more funny than tragic, but the real goals that we would try to serve may be set back by it nonetheless.

An optimistic generation at the beginning of the twentieth century had to learn to not identify their plans too closely with the will of God, and we have learned that lesson from them well. We should not forget it as we enter into a new century, but we may also need to learn that without a plan of some sort to connect us to the largest goals for which we hope, we may never get around to planning for more than our retirement. People of faith must be aware that God may interrupt their plans and send them in a new direction, but we cannot change direction unless we are already going someplace.

It is only by making plans that I can connect my life in a practical way to the larger goals that reach beyond it. I may have an intellectual understanding of peace and justice and a theology that relates those purposes to God's action in history. So I will be able to speak quite persuasively about these topics when they come up for discussion. If I am good enough at it and learn enough about it, I may become a theologian or a preacher. I may even write a book about ethics. But unless those larger goals that are in some special way God's goals connect to my goals *in action*, those larger goals are in no way part of my moral life, no matter how large they may be in my thinking and dreaming.

A plan is not the goal. We need room for spontaneity that comes from new inspiration or new relationships, and we lose that when we insist always on following the plan. Above all, when the goals are large and lasting, we need opportunities for self-correction and renewal that come from thinking through our plans in light of the way that others are working toward the same goal. If we cannot distinguish our plans from the goal, we will end up identifying anyone who is working toward the same goal by a different way as an enemy, and we will be locked into whatever mistakes we have made in our own way of working.

A plan is not the goal, but a plan is an essential part of having a real goal. A plan is not a picture of how the future must be. A plan is about what I am going to do today in relation to a goal that may lie many years in the future, well beyond the boundaries of my life and work. I make plans not as predictions about a distant future, but as commitments about my actions in the present.

A plan is also a way to make my commitments available to others. If I have a plan, people can rely on what I will do; but a plan also gives them an opportunity to challenge me and make objections to my way of moving toward the goal. Often they will object, not by rejecting my goal, but by saying that this is not the right way to go about achieving the goal. There are things that we should not do, even in order to get to a result that is important and good.

When we begin that sort of discussion, the argument turns quickly to talk about rules. Someone proposes to get the money for renovating the day care center by investing the building fund in the stock market, and someone else quickly points out that there are rules against that. We try to cut expenses by using less expensive materials, and we learn about building codes and licensing standards. Thinking about what we should and should not do on our way to a goal involves us in making, testing, and using rules. And that will take us, in the next chapter, to the second major way of thinking about ethics.

CHAPTER 3

Rules

For some people, rules are the most important part of ethics. Of course, we are all interested in a good life, these people would say, but the good life and its goals are morally important because there are rules that tell us which goals we should choose and what kind of life we ought to live. Goals, like tastes in food or music, are individual and personal. Rules have to be objective and apply to everybody.

Other people think that the emphasis on rules is mistaken. What we are really concerned about in ethics, they say, are the qualities that we admire in other people and hope to make a part of our own lives. We are careful to observe the rules when we know that the authorities are watching, but goals and virtues are what we really care about. We like to regard the rules as objective and permanent, especially when we are enforcing them on somebody else; but in reality the rules are constantly changing. What endures are the qualities of people that are worth honoring and emulating.

Each of these approaches to moral rules has found its way into Christian ethics; and each, taken by itself, is too simple. Periodically, religious leaders become concerned that Christians are too legalistic and inflexible, applying moral rules rigidly and driving people away from churches with their judgmental attitudes. When that mood prevails, some ethicists will begin to speak of a Christian ethics without rules or where the only rule is to do the most loving thing. More recently some observers have seen the decline of respect for moral rules as part of a serious erosion of life in American society, and Christian conservatives have begun to call for more rigorous individual observance of moral rules and even for enacting some of these moral requirements into law.

It is unlikely that we will do more than bounce back and forth between these two unsatisfactory extremes unless we can incorporate moral rules into a more comprehensive understanding of the Christian life. That understanding will include the recognition of moral rules as an expression of God's will and rule over human life, but it will also take account of other ways that God's will is known. It will recognize that in the biblical faith rules are obeyed or broken in the context of a community. That community helps us to understand what obedience to the rule requires, suffers the consequences along with the individual when the rule is broken, and sustains the possibility of repentance and reconciliation through which broken relationships can be restored. When we have arrived at this more comprehensive understanding of the place of moral rules in Christian ethics, we will be in a better position to say what the rules can and cannot do and how they are related to goals and to the search for the good life that we have examined in chapters 1 and 2.

Deontology

Before we turn to understandings of rules that are specific to Christian ethics, we need to learn some terms that are commonly used in contemporary studies of ethics. This will help us be more clear about stating the alternatives in Christian thought.

Philosophers speak of a system of ethics that is based on rules as a *deontology* or as a *deontological ethics.* The term is derived from a Greek root, *deon,* which concerns that which is necessary or required. Deontological ethics makes doing one's duty, doing what is required, the key determinant of whether one is a good person.[1] Deontological ethics evaluates actions by asking whether this action was the right thing to do according to a rule, not by assessing what happens as the result of the action. A church treasurer who follows the rule that says the endowment fund is to be invested only in government bonds has done the right thing, even if the church could make a great deal more money with relatively little risk by a short-term investment in the stock market. A prosecutor who follows the letter of the law and indicts a local businessman for a minor crime has done the right thing, even if the subsequent conviction results in great hardship for the offender's employees and economic losses to the entire community. Results, the deontologists remind us, are often unpredictable and largely out of our control. Our moral assessment of ourselves and others has to rest on more secure ground. Rules provide a stable and certain starting point for our moral evaluations.

Even the most rigorous deontologist has to admit, however, that applying the rules is not simple. We all remember encounters with stern teachers and stubborn bureaucrats who thought that it was easy to say what the rules are, but those people were not ethicists. Ethicists recognize that we are subject to many different systems of rules and that these systems are sometimes in conflict.

Within each of the systems, moreover, some rules are more important than others. Most systems of rules make a distinction between *rules,* which are specific standards of conduct, and *principles,* which state the broader guidelines on which the rules are based. The concepts of "stewardship" and "community," discussed in chapter 2, are examples of principles in Christian ethics. Most thoughtful Christians would agree that these principles are important guides to Christian conduct, but there is room for considerable debate about exactly what actions they require. Indeed, people who adhere to the same principles may derive different and opposing rules from them. A principle that says that private property should be respected may take the form of a rule that forbids the neighbors from walking their dogs on a vacant lot that is posted with "no trespassing" signs, but the same principle may also forbid the owner of the lot from putting up an ugly fence that diminishes the neighbors' enjoyment of their own property.

Those who build their ethics on rules usually know that making, knowing, and applying the rules are not simple things to do. But they believe that the distinction between right and wrong in action is more important and easier to determine than the difference between good and bad results. An ethics based on rules, a deontological ethics, will not give us what we often believe we want when we start thinking about moral rules. It will not give us a set of simple rules that apply in every situation whatsoever. Human life and the decisions people have to make are too complicated for that. But it is possible to develop a system of ethics in which rules are the most important determinants of right and wrong in actions. It may be hard to decide how to apply a general rule about telling the truth to the difficult problem of how to talk to a patient about a life-threatening illness, but many people think that the rule to tell the truth is important precisely because it forces us to face that difficult problem rather than settling for what takes less of the physician's time or saying what we think the patient wants to hear. It may be difficult to know exactly where one person's rights end and another person's freedom begins, but many people think that it is easier to define and to apply the rules that make up a system of rights and duties than to get everyone in society working toward a common goal that might make the rules unnecessary.

Simple arrangements to share resources or facilities often work primarily by rules. We all have encountered lists of rules posted at the entrance to a park or a beach or over the sink in the office break room. Many of us live in condominium apartments or housing developments that require everyone to observe certain regulations while using shared space. Professional ethics are often deontological systems. Doctors, lawyers, accountants, social workers, and other professional groups each have a code of ethics that sets down rules for people in the profession to follow in dealing with one another and with clients. Usually the code also states general principles by which the rules are to be interpreted and sets up procedures to determine how they should be applied, but the rules are the heart of the system. Modern systems of constitutional law and democratic government are often understood as deontological systems too. Constitutional principles determine who can make laws and what sorts of laws can be made, and courts make complex decisions about how the laws are to be applied; but no one doubts that the laws determine what should and should not be done, not the goals of the leaders or the wishes of the majority.

So we all have some experience of deontological ethics. The question is whether Christian ethics, too, is a system in which the rules are primary.

Divine Command Ethics

Those who understand Christian ethics as deontological ethics stress the importance of obeying God's commandments in the life of faith. Obviously, what makes these rules important is that they are *God's* rules. The Hebrew scriptures surround the giving of the law to Moses with the awesome image of God giving direct orders to the people. How they are to worship, how they are to treat one another, and how they are to live their daily lives are prescribed by rules that are important because they are given by God (Exod 20:1-17). In the New Testament Jesus speaks of the importance of following these laws as they were given (Mark 7:6-13) and denies that he intends to abolish them (Matt 5:17-20). For Christians, it is important to separate God's genuine commandments from human traditions that weaken or distort them; but once those distinctions are made, the central importance of obeying God shapes the Christian life.

Christian thinking that develops a deontological ethics based on the commandments of God as recorded in Scripture is often called a "divine command" ethics. For this way of thinking, the emphasis on God's commandments is important not just because these rules come from God, but also because there is no other reliable way to know and understand God's will. Although all Christians would affirm that it is important to seek God's will for our lives and to live according to our understanding of it, divine command ethics adds to this the claim that the rules set forth in Scripture as God's commandments are the only way to know what God's will is. People may speak about seeing God's plan in nature or about learning God's plan for their lives in their own experience; but strictly speaking, for the divine command ethicist, these ways of speaking are mistaken. If we truly know God's will, it is because we have understood these other places where we think we find it through what

44

we know of God's commandments in Scripture. Our human reasoning is so limited and so apt to be distorted by what we want or what we wish for others that the only way for us to know what God wants us to do is for God to tell us. That is why the rules set out in God's commandments are central to Christian ethics. Rules are the way that God has chosen to speak to us. There may be other ways to set goals and make decisions about action, but they cannot be *Christian* ethics.

While preachers and prophets across the centuries have called people to follow the commandments of God, it has been Protestant thinkers in the twentieth century who have most consistently developed divine command theory as a systematic way of thinking about Christian ethics. In keeping with the Protestant emphasis on Scripture as the sole authoritative Word of God and the early Reformers' caution against setting up any other authorities or intermediaries between the Christian and God, Protestant theologians have tried to root out other authorities and sources from the Christian understanding of right and wrong.

Divine command theory is one way to understand the place of rules in Christian ethics, but it is not the only way. Some regard the exclusive emphasis on rules as too narrow an understanding of what the Scriptures tell us about God's will and how it is known, and critics point out that we are as likely to read our own desires and prejudices into our statements about what God wants as we are to impose them on the way we see God's plan in nature or at work in our experience. Human sin and weakness often distorts our understanding of God's will, but divine command theorists are no more immune to these distortions than is anyone else. Our choices for thinking about Christian ethics are not so simple as accepting the divine command account of the rules or rejecting rules altogether. But we need to consider some other ways in which rules can be important in Christian ethics.

Natural Law

In the New Testament Jesus criticizes the narrow emphasis on religious rules not only because it sometimes substitutes human goals for God's purposes, but also because it separates God's rules from God's purposes, neglecting the healing and wholeness that God intends for human life in favor of restrictions about when to heal and how to do good (John 7:19-24). Jesus likens himself to a shepherd who devotes his life to protecting the sheep from predators, healing their injuries, and seeing that they have food and water. He says that he has come to give life and to give it abundantly (John 10:10).

In this context the distinction that divine command ethics makes between God's rules and human goals begins to lose its sharpness. God has purposes for human life too; and although we are often mistaken about what is really good for us, the abundant life God wants for us cannot be completely different from our own understanding of what a good life would be.

Wanting abundant life and knowing how to get it, however, can be two quite different things. We often charge in directly after things we want, without thinking about what we need to do to enjoy them safely or to have them securely for the future. We are apt to mistake superficial signs of abundance—possessions, power, and opportunities—for a true enjoyment of life that enriches us with relationships to others and enables us to grow in understanding of ourselves and knowledge of the world around us. The things that make for a good life are not always the first things we want, and often what we really need can be achieved only through a discipline that can seem like a burden for a long time before we begin to understand its benefits. So we need rules, if only to direct us to the goals that are really worth pursuing.

People learn such rules by experience, by bumping up against the limits of their human capacities, or by learning how they have to behave to get along with their neighbors. Proverbs, fables, and rules are passed along from generation to generation, but usually with the wry sense that no matter how cleverly the elders put it, each generation has to make its own mistakes and learn this wisdom for itself.

These traditions are ancient. The early Christians were familiar with the "wisdom literature" of the Hebrew scriptures, especially the books of Proverbs and Ecclesiastes, which they traced back to the much older time of the kingdom of Israel. But they knew that there were similar traditions, some of them thought to be even older, among the many peoples and religions who crowded along with them into the cities of the Roman Empire. For Christian and Jewish writers, the way the natural world seemed to teach this wisdom for living could not be separated from their conviction that the order of that world is the work of God's creation. Much of what Scripture teaches clearly as the command of God can also be learned by people who are paying attention to their own experience, whether they know the Scriptures or not. Paul explained it in his letter to the Romans this way: "When Gentiles, who do not possess the law, do instinctively what the law requires, these, though not having the law, are a law to themselves. They show that what the law requires is written on their hearts" (Rom 2:14-15*a*).

Eventually, this effort to relate common human wisdom to a more basic order established by God in creation took the form of a fully developed theory of *natural law*. Natural law ethics is probably the oldest systematic form of Christian ethics, a deontological system in which the basic rules are known by everyone through life's experiences. People find out for themselves what will and will not work in the order of things in which everyone must live, and learn to live together. These rules are not natural laws in the sense that modern science speaks of the law of gravity, which controls all of our actions whether we think about it or not. The moral law is something that we can either keep or break in making our decisions. We have to think about it to follow it. But the moral law is "natural" in the sense that it is part of who we are and of the world we live in, so that its requirements are inescapable. Natural law does not apply to us because we are citizens of a particular country or believers in a certain religion or because we have been taught a certain set of moral rules. It applies to us because we are human. This has the important implication that no one can escape judgment by its standards. It may be hard for people to agree on exactly what the natural law requires or forbids; but if they can agree, they can also hold people accountable to it. To say that they did not know the natural law or that they do not accept its authority or that the laws of their country or their religion set different rules will not excuse them.

Accounts of what the natural law requires usually begin with basic patterns of human development and human relationships. We cannot live without developing habits that secure our health and well-being, and we cannot live together without reliable cooperation with others; therefore, the requirements of self-restraint, developing our own abilities, and keeping the promises we make to others are among the generally recognized principles of natural law. Human beings come especially close to the biological requirements for survival and thriving in those intimate relations in which families are created and children are nurtured; consequently, sexuality and the relationships between parents and children are often understood in terms of natural law, although it is especially difficult to separate the requirements of nature from the expectations of culture in this area. Perhaps the most basic requirement of nature is that we recognize others as people like ourselves, vulnerable to the limitations of our fragile humanity, but also capable creating communities in which that humanity is nurtured and creates new possibilities. Natural law recognizes these shared needs and also respects the dignity we share just because we are human; thus the rules of natural law become the starting point for human rights.

Ideas about natural law become important when people find that they have to live together in situations where they lack shared goals and shared traditions that shape their expectations of one another. The idea that some things are right "by nature" is found already in Aristotle.[2] Stoic philosophers and Roman lawyers developed this idea to suit the needs of a large, diverse empire. Cicero (106–43 BCE) spoke of a law that is not one law in Athens and another in Rome, but the same everywhere because it is written into the structure of reality. Paul's letter to the Romans, as we have seen, speaks of a similar law that is known to every human conscience. It is uncertain whether Paul knew the philosophical theories that echo his formulations, but later Christian writers explicitly adopted the ideas of Cicero and other Stoic philosophers, so that the "law of nature" became a common theme in Christian thought as well.

In the Middle Ages Thomas Aquinas (1125–74) developed a synthesis of Christian and classical learning that clearly connected the natural law to God's commandments.[3] As European explorers in the early sixteenth century began to encounter civilizations and peoples previously unknown to them, Bartolomé de Las Casas (1474–1566) and other religious leaders used these natural law ideas to argue against the exploitation of the native peoples of the Americas. Thinking about natural law declined as scientific understandings of nature began to replace Aristotelian philosophy at the beginning of the modern era; but during the course of the twentieth century, as military aggression, nationalism, and genocide have all taken their toll on human life, theologians, philosophers, and international lawyers have rediscovered the importance of identifying some moral expectations that can be imposed on everyone and some forms of moral respect from which no one can be excluded on grounds of race, religion, or ethnicity.

The idea of natural law remains controversial in contemporary Christian ethics. It is easy to say that there must be some standards that apply to all human cultures, and difficult to say exactly what those standards are. When people confuse their own experience with human experience in general, an appeal to natural law may make it easier for them to vilify those who are different from themselves, branding their actions or their culture as "unnatural," and justifying persecution of those who fail to comply with the requirements of nature as the dominant group understands them. In the hands of an authority that claims exclusive knowledge of what is and is not "natural," natural law easily becomes an instrument of abuse or oppression.

But the idea behind natural law does not lend itself easily to such one-way interpretations. The idea of natural law is to seek human unity in spite of obvious differences. Despite all the many forms of culture that human beings have created and the many different rules by which they live, natural law reminds us that there are some human needs that we have in common and some constraints in nature that we must take seriously if we are to survive and thrive. There are many different ideas about human good, and we are constantly discovering new ones as our experience of other people and other cultures grows. The variety is vast, but it is not infinite.

By paying attention to the physical and biological needs that human organisms share, seeking to understand how individuals develop abilities and personalities that satisfy those needs, and taking account of the forms of cooperation that bind human communities together and enable them to survive through time, we can come to some basic agreements about what human nature requires. Those requirements, in turn, provide the basis for a set of rules about how we should treat one another in order to respect each person's humanity as well as our own. If these rules are not sufficient to describe a complete moral life, they at least provide the essentials on which we can agree across differences of culture, tradition, and individual desires. It is not easy to develop this consensus, but without it there is no moral accountability that extends beyond the boundaries of my own group. Power alone determines whose view will prevail.

It is because they are unwilling to accept the alternative that "might makes right" that many philosophers and legal theorists have developed new proposals for natural law in the last half of the twentieth century. Christian ethicists also participate in this exploration of the moral imperatives that are inherent in the human condition. Some do so reluctantly because they believe that human needs are easily confused with human desires and they prefer to trust the commandments articulated in Scripture rather than formulate a natural law. Others take up the idea of natural law with enthusiasm. They believe that the requirements of human life that all of us can explore together are also an expression of the will of God as it is made known in God's creation. What Scripture and tradition tell us about God's will helps us to understand our experience of human life and human possibilities, but the things we learn from that experience also help us to interpret what Scripture and tradition tell us about God's will. Our knowledge of ecology and our awareness of the impact that human beings have on the delicate balances of nature forces us to rethink the biblical idea that God has given human beings dominion over nature. We understand ourselves today more as stewards of God's order and less as masters of it. Because we understand that mental illness has physiological causes and sometimes genetic origins, we relate differently to those who suffer from it than our ancestors did when they understood it as God's punishment for some personal fault or failing.

These new ideas inevitably change the moral rules that we apply in our dealings with other people and with nature. For the Christian who accepts some version of natural law ethics, these changes are part of a growing understanding of God's will known through God's creation. As our knowledge of the world grows and our contact with people who have cultures and ideas different from our own becomes more and more a daily occurrence, this ability to rethink what is morally required of us in light of new knowledge and new experience will surely be more and more needed. Natural law ethics, the oldest systematic form of Christian moral thinking, has a place in the future of Christian ethics too.

Covenant and Rules

We spoke in chapter 2 of the covenant commitments that can bind persons together in the pursuit of goals that are important to each of them. These covenant commitments provide another way to understand moral rules that is prominent in Scripture and in both Christian and Jewish traditions. The key example in the Bible is the covenant God makes with the people of Israel at Mount Sinai. God has delivered the people from slavery in Egypt and promised to bring them into a land of their own. But there is more to the relationship than God's actions and promises. The covenant comes into being when Moses delivers God's law and the people promise to obey it (Exodus 19–20).

The covenant is more than just a set of rules. It is a relationship of lasting commitment in which upholding the rules is a part of faithfulness to the covenant. Indeed, Israel's prophets would later identify *hesed*, steadfast love, as the thing that holds the covenant together, so that even when the rules are broken by the people's disobedience, God's faithfulness holds the covenant in being. It is not keeping the rules that makes a covenant. If that were strictly required, no covenant would last for very long. What makes a covenant is having the rules and acknowledging that they are important and that they remain a part of who we are, even when we do not keep them.

Natural law locates the moral rules in an order that is part of reality. Covenant thinking locates them in a relationship of faithfulness between people or between individuals and God. Without this steadfast love the rules taken by themselves have little meaning. Of course, we have a sentimental notion that the deeper love goes, the less the rules matter; but the covenant tradition is wiser than our soap operas and romance novels on this point. In faithful relationships we know what to expect from our partners and what they may ask of us. Rules spell out the terms of the relationship. We may not always keep them, and that will require a love that goes beyond mere obedience. But if we are left guessing about what this relationship offers, what it may require of us, and when it is apt to end, we hardly have a relationship at all. Knowing the rules makes covenant faithfulness possible.

Unlike natural law, which is an inquiry into the rules that all human beings share, covenant rules often require more specific things of us and impose obligations that are not universal. Covenant rules establish a particular identity and community within the wider human family. Jews who follow rabbinic law about diet, dress, and daily habits are identified as participants in the covenant by their adherence to these rules. The same is true for very traditional Christians, like the Amish, whose distinctive dress and rejection of modern technology and culture identifies them as part of a particular Christian community. Most Christians—and many Jews—do not follow their faith covenant in a way that would distinguish them so sharply from their neighbors, but they still follow rules that mark them out as people who belong to a particular covenant. Christians set aside time on Sunday morning, and perhaps other times of the week as well, to gather with others for worship. They pause for prayer before meals or at the beginning of a meeting. They practice stewardship of their financial resources, and they take seriously their obligation to help those in need, not only with their money, but with their time. Especially in the way they organize their family lives, they say to one another and to the rest of the world, "We know that there are other ways to order our lives, but these are the rules that we follow because we are part of the Christian covenant." Covenant rules include the minimal requirements for successful human living that all persons share. That is what links covenant ethics to natural law. But covenant rules go beyond this minimum to establish additional rules that identify the members of this covenant and specify the things they expect of one another.

Such covenants establish faithfulness between people as well as relationships with God. The covenant idea, especially as it was lived out in the congregational communities of English settlers in North America, had a profound influence on our modern ideas of democratic government. In the United States, law depends on the will of the people, but it is not just an arbitrary list of the rules the majority happens to want. Laws are made in the framework of a more basic relationship—a covenant, if you will—that is spelled out in the Constitution. The rights the Constitution prescribes may be justified by an appeal to the laws of nature, but these rights become effective because we are committed to a system of rules that require us to observe these rights in the actions of our goverment and in our dealings with one another. Commitment to constitutional government implies not just a recognition of the basic human rights that ought to be observed everywhere, but also a commitment to follow the laws and procedures that this constitutional system has set up, even though we understand that other rules are possible.

Covenants and Contracts

Participation in a covenant community requires a deep personal commitment to others who are part of the covenant, even when its rules may not be the ones we would have chosen for ourselves. In that, covenant community differs sharply from another understanding of human relationships that has also influenced modern democracy, the idea of a *social contract.* Contracts are commitments that individuals make with one another because each sees the relationship in his or her own self-interest. If I agree to sell you sixty bushels of wheat in four months at a set price, it is because I think I will have that much wheat to spare at the end of the time and that I will gain more by having your money than I would by keeping the wheat. Your needs and goals are not a part of my calculation, and I may even break the agreement if it turns out in four months' time that I would gain more by breaking it than it would cost me to compensate you for your loss.

As this sort of commerce grew at the beginning of the modern era, philosophers saw it as a model not only for business relationships, but for the creation of society. People come together to form governments and subject themselves to laws because they gain more by living with the restraints of law than they would lose by risking themselves to a "state of nature" in which there was no authority with power to keep order, protect rights, and enforce agreements. Although the governments and laws under which individuals live today may have been in place for generations, philosophers tried to show that these laws could have been the result of that sort of calculation of self-interest and that the consent of today's citizens rests on that same sort of understanding. Of course, it was easier to make this case when people moved from the old kingdoms of Europe to new settlements in North America and established systems of government that were set up in their own lifetimes.[4] Perhaps most important for the revolutionary thinkers who led the movements toward democracy in Europe and North America at the end of the eighteenth century, the social contract theory implied that when patterns of law and government arise that cannot be justified by the individual consent of citizens who are thinking about their own self-interest, those governments may be set aside by the people.

Social contract, then, suggests that we follow rules because we have in some sense chosen them. We may not always like what they require of us; but when we consider the matter rationally, we will find that we prefer those requirements to the alternatives. Despite the popularity of this idea in American philosophy and politics, the earlier concept of covenant seems a better explanation of the power of those rules that are most important to us. In a covenant the rules are part of a relationship, not just a way of securing our own best interests. It simplifies matters to say that the rules are the ones we would have chosen if we had taken time to think about it. The more complicated truth seems to be that the rules are part of a relationship that defines us and makes us who we are, so that even if I decide that I cannot accept some part of the rules, they continue to be a part of my identity and make a claim on my actions. I cannot escape the rules that are part of a covenantal relationship as easily as I can renegotiate or break the terms of a contract that turn out not to be in my own self-interest.

Covenantal traditions provide for change, not by setting aside relationships that prove unsatisfactory, but by distinguishing between the rules that are central to the covenant and those that are interpretations and applications of the more basic rules to new conditions and changing circumstances. The Jewish people have sustained their covenant over many centuries through rabbinic interpretations that restate Torah as *halakah,* the commandments that Jews follow in their daily walk where they happen to be living now. Protestant Reformers, who gave new emphasis to covenant and to God's commandments in place of the natural law theories of late medieval Christianity, recognized that alongside the basics of church teaching and Christian living that they tried to discern in Scripture, there were many things that were *adiaphora,* matters that could be decided in different ways by different Christian groups, each being faithful in its own way to the central truths of Christian faith. Political systems based on the rule of law distinguish between ordinary legislation and the constitutional principles on which that legislation is based.

Life in a covenant community, then, does not require that one accept all of its rules just as they are. That expectation may, in fact, be more appropriate to a social contract, where you either agree that the rules are in your best interest or you do not; and if you do not, there is not much reason for you to be there. In a covenant community there is a continuing relationship to others in the covenant, and, in a religious covenant, continuing faithfulness to God, who calls the covenant community into being. Part of life in the covenant is learning what is central to its relationships and what is peripheral, what is the commandment of God that makes the covenant people who they are and what is part of the changing ways that this people have tried to walk in faith in different times and places. It is, in fact, by questioning the rules while remaining faithful to the relationship that we find out what is central to the covenant.

Covenant does not preclude interpretations of ancient rules that help us to understand what they mean in new circumstances. What covenant precludes is an individualistic approach to this interpretative task that examines the rules and decides what to keep and what to discard according to one's own set of values and then acts on those decisions without regard for others. Interpretation in a covenant community always involves a great deal of listening, and the decision to act must involve choices not only about what is right and what is wrong, but also about what course of action will sustain this process of communication for the future. The decision to leave a covenant is not made by deciding to do this thing rather than that. It is made by deciding to not try anymore to understand or to persuade.

Rules and Goals

We are now in a position to take another look at the question about how rules and goals are related, with which we began this chapter. Christian ethics has at least three ways to understand moral rules: as God's commandments, as the requirements of natural law, and as part of a covenant that includes relationships to God and to other people. These three understandings are not incompatible. The rule against murder, for example, is one that the Bible presents as directly commanded by God. It is also understood as an act that people everywhere recognize as wrong, as a violation of their consciences and of the natural order of relationships between human beings. The rule is also part of the covenant relationship, in which a long tradition of interpretation and reinterpretation helps people to understand exactly what it means.

The emphasis in each way of thinking about rules is different, however. Speaking of the rules as God's commandments stresses that it is God's authority that makes the distinction between right and wrong and God's revelation that allows us to know which is which. Natural law thinking emphasizes the connection between how we live as thoughtful, reasonable human beings and the natural order in which God has placed all of us. An emphasis on covenantal relationships calls attention to how the rules shape our identity as persons in community. Depending on where you place the emphasis, you may find different rules important for Christian living; and if you stress one understanding of rules exclusively, you may even conclude that the other ways of thinking are not Christian at all. Most of us, however, make some use of all three ways of thinking about the rules that we follow in Christian living.

What the three ways of thinking about rules seem to have in common is the idea that important moral rules are objective. They do not depend on our goals and choices. We are obliged to follow them whether or not their requirements fit with our preferences, our goals, or our sense of who we want to be. Moral rules exist independently of our thinking about them, in the will of God, in the order of nature, in the life of the covenant community. To be sure, there are some rules that are just our rules. You want your children to learn to appreciate the skills involved in making music, so you set a rule that they must practice the piano for half an hour every day. My university has rules about choosing airline flights and rental car companies in order to keep travel costs down. Moral rules are not quite like that. They are more than convenient ways of keeping track of my goals or telling other people what they must do in order to achieve a goal. Moral rules set limits on all of our choices and goals. Without them we have only plans, not ethics.

Because moral rules are independent of our preferences and goals in this way, they serve several functions in our moral thinking. First, rules tell us what we may not do on the way to achieving our goals. Having goals is essential to living a good life, as we have seen in chapter 2, and a good goal will justify many personal sacrifices and many demands on other people in order to achieve it. But it will not justify everything. At some point, the goal of becoming a physician or a scholar and using the gifts of healing and knowledge to help other people shades over into an obsession that subordinates normal caring for other people to the goal's demands, and sacrifices the good life of individuals to the good life imagined in the goal. Rules help us to identify the thin line that separates our goals, with their necessary sacrifices, from obsessions that can destroy us and others with their excessive demands. We may not steal the resources that belong to another person in order to achieve our good goals. We may not lie to obtain what we want, even if what we want is a very good thing. We may not coerce others into helping us with our goals against their will, or threaten them with harm if they get in the way of our achieving the good things we want to do.

All of this may seem obvious when it is stated so plainly. Most of us are clear that we cannot go around lying, cheating, and beating up on other people just to achieve our goals. We may be tempted to do these things under extreme pressure or stress, but we are not likely to think that they are good things to do. It is harder to remember this, however, when the goals are really big ones that reach beyond our personal desires and plans. It is much easier to think that the spread of true religion or the survival of my nation or the advancement of science is so important that it justifies whatever I might have to do to other people to make it possible. Perhaps the most important thing that rules do in any system of ethics is to warn us not to think in that way. The more obviously good our goals are and the more earnestly we are committed to them, the more we need to be reminded of what we may not do in order to achieve them.

A second function rules have in the moral life is that they establish disciplines that are important in our personal lives. Rules set boundaries within which our personal choices are made and establish an overall structure for our days and weeks within which we plan our activities. A rule that establishes that we should give a percentage of our income to help meet the needs of the poor sets a baseline for all the rest of our financial planning. A rule that prescribes a time of worship on Sunday morning or a daily time of prayer at the beginning and the end of the day helps to structure all of our time and keeps us mindful of a relationship to God that we might otherwise forget amidst the distractions of our goal-oriented activities. For some groups, rules about dress or diet are important signs of religious identity. Obeying those rules reminds both observant members and outsiders who these people are and what their faith expects of them. In a society where temptations to overconsumption are almost always at hand, we each need our own rules about what to eat, what to drink, and what to wear in order to keep our impulses from getting the better of us. These rules may seem purely personal, even quirky, but they serve an important moral purpose if they enable us to do good things that our goals and our desires alone would not sustain.

Over time, rules that provide personal discipline shape our lives as powerfully as do our goals. Goals change, sometimes dramatically. Often it is the rules that provide continuity. Familiar rituals at worship or patterns of private prayer can sustain us when the life we have structured around our goals comes unglued and the goals themselves all have to be rethought. Personal disciplines—exercise, diet, thrift—have their most important effects over the long run, when we keep them up through a lifetime of changes. Who we are is the result of the rules we have followed as surely as it can be seen in the goals we pursue.

Of course, the rules become most effective in our lives when we have followed them so consistently that we do not particularly need to think about them. We may begin by writing down our rules and consulting the list regularly or by buying a book that gives us the rules of effective leadership or positive parenting or even continuing spiritual growth. Whatever rules we follow, we occasionally need time to step back and examine our lives reflectively, to see how we are really doing at keeping the rules we say we accept. But most of the time the rules need to be part of us. We cannot follow them effectively if we have to be constantly flipping through the rule book to find the one that applies. Rules have to become habits or *virtues* if they are to be effective personal disciplines. (We will look at this relationship between rules and virtues more closely in the next chapter.)

A third use of rules is that rules form communities. It might seem that common goals are the most important thing for a community of people to share, but we learn rather quickly in experience that goals alone do not produce real community. In addition to the assurance that others want some of the same things that we want, we need some specific understandings about what they will and will not do if we are to live and work together with them toward the goals that we share. It is no accident that the *Rule of St. Benedict,* which has guided life in monasteries since the early Middle Ages, begins with a prologue about the goal of the

Christian life and then works its way through seventy-three chapters of sometimes very specific rules about eating, working, and praying together. Contemporary Christians who are not at all monastic often find the *Rule* an important guide to Christian life precisely because of the wisdom it contains about the rules we have to follow in the details of everyday matters if we are to live in community with others and achieve the great things we say we want to do together.

The rules in our communities where we work, in our churches, and in our neighborhoods are rarely written down with the precision of the *Rule of St. Benedict,* but we know what the rules are nonetheless. We recognize a violation when we see it, and learning what the rules are is an important part of becoming a member of the community. We recognize shared values and a certain relationship with other people who share our goals; but if we are actually going to live and work with them, we will also need some rules.

Conclusion

Rules have a central place in the moral life, but they are not the whole of it. Rules provide a kind of architecture of the moral life. Knowing the rules is a way of understanding how our choices about the good life have to be structured. If we ignore them, we may build a way of life that is superficially attractive and gets us things that we want in the short run, but that will collapse under its own weight long before we arrive at the happiness in relationships with God and with other people that is the real goal of the moral life. To change the metaphor, rules mark out roads or pathways in the moral life. Like a road map, they offer us many choices about how to travel, but they do this precisely by limiting our choices: At this intersection, you may turn left or right, but you should not strike out across the field in hope of getting to your destination by a more direct route than the roads provide. Often we are more interested in the destination than in the route we are going to travel, but it would be a mistake to ignore the map or to think that how you proceed toward your destination has no bearing on when you are likely to get there or what shape you will be in when you arrive.

Rules provide structure for the moral life, but they cannot live it for us. Rules cannot choose our goals for us, nor can strict obedience to the rules substitute for a commitment to the goals and to the personal disciplines that are required to reach them.

We need to remember this when we want to provide leadership in dealing with ethical issues where we work or in our communities. Too often we suppose that the only way to speak up for higher moral standards is to remind people of the rules they are breaking. We tell manufacturers that they should not lie to their customers about the safety of the products they make. We tell unwed fathers that they have a responsibility for their children. We tell government officials that they must not use their public power as an opportunity for private gain. Those basic moral rules are important, and it takes some courage to stand up for them at times when most people find it more convenient to ignore them. But reminding people of the rules rarely solves the problem by itself. Managers lie to their bosses and businesses lie to the public because they do not have a goal that goes beyond protecting themselves from the consequences of their mistakes or making a short-term profit for the company. People slide into addictions and ignore their responsibilities to their families when they have lost hope for themselves and their future. They begin to deal drugs and exploit the needs of their neighbors when they do not see any goal in life that offers a realistic promise of something better. They charge exorbitant prices for shoddy merchandise and substandard housing when they do not feel that they are part of the same human community with the people they are cheating.

It is often very satisfying to denounce these abuses and the people who commit them. Calling attention to the offense may stop some of the worst problems or at least lead the offenders to take their mischief elsewhere. But it is unlikely really to change anyone; and once the spotlight is switched off, the problems are apt to return. A genuine effort at moral reform will see to it that the people who are now breaking the rules have an opportunity to form goals that are worth living for within the structures of life that moral rules provide. It will worry about their aspirations as well as criticizing their actions. A genuine effort at moral reform seeks to build community, so that those who now find it necessary—or perhaps just convenient—to exploit their neighbors will have reasons to respect them and to cooperate with them for goals that the whole community shares.

That way of seeking higher moral standards is more demanding than a simple reiteration of the rules, but it is also more realistic about what the moral life requires. Insisting on obedience to the rules is not likely to be successful all by itself because people need goals and community as well as rules in order to live a moral life. Unless we provide opportunities for those aspects of the moral life to flourish, along with our exhortations to live within the structures that the moral rules provide, we are unlikely to produce lasting change in people or in our communities.

We have to remember the limitations of moral rules in our own lives as well. Rules provide structure for the moral life; but simply following the rules is not living morally—and it certainly isn't living well. We've all had experience of people who seek to live their lives by keeping all the rules and giving offense to no one. Their conduct may be impeccable, but we do not find them to be models for the way we would want to live. They seem to have lost the center of their lives in their efforts to conform to everyone else's expectations. We find nothing in them to criticize, but we have the uncomfortable feeling that something is missing. It may be that they have no goals beyond avoiding other people's disapproval or that they have no real sense of community with the people whose rules they are so careful to keep.

We run into similar problems with the institutions of which we are a part—businesses, churches, community organizations, and governmental agencies. Each of these exists in a regulatory environment that is increasingly complex and detailed. An older pattern that built on handshake agreements between individuals and left wide areas to the discretion of owners, managers, and public officials now gives way to a system of laws, regulations, codes of ethics, and public disclosure that limits action at every point. Those who make decisions for the institution must depend on advice from lawyers, compliance officers, and public relations counsels as well as their own judgments about the best way to achieve the goals for which they are working.

These regulations are important, morally as well as legally. They require us to pay attention to the health and safety of the people who work in our businesses. They keep us from perpetuating patterns of race and gender discrimination that stubbornly resist our good intentions for change. They require us to take down the physical and procedural barriers that prevent people with disabilities from achieving the fullness of life of which they are capable. They assure the public that they can trust the quality of what we offer them, whether that is fish or financial advice, education, health care, or used cars. We cannot ignore the structure that these rules provide for our institutional lives, not just because breaking the rules results in complaints, investigations, fines, and lots of paperwork, but because the rules are morally important.

But in our institutions, as in our individual lives, just keeping the rules is not enough. Our schools, churches, and businesses need goals in order to flourish, just as we need goals in our individual lives. An institution that simply lives within the rules probably will not do much harm, but it will not accomplish much good either; and it may not be able to sustain the personal commitments that will be required if the institution is to survive and carry on its work into the future.

Rules, we have observed, tell us what we should not do on the way to achieving our goals. What this means is that rules and goals, far from being mutually exclusive and independent ways of organizing the moral life, are, in fact, dependent on one another. Moral rules only make sense as a structure or framework for the pursuit of morally important goals.

Moral goals will destroy the happiness they seek if they are pursued without the restraint provided by moral rules. History offers us many examples of persons and institutions that were destroyed morally by an unlimited ambition for goals that broke down the rules and rights of others. Examples of the opposite error, sacrificing worthwhile goals to the constraints of overly narrow rules, are less dramatic, but they are probably more numerous. Unless we have a passion for some goals in our individual lives and some sense of mission in our institutions that leads us to test what the framework of the rules will allow, we probably will not have much of a moral life, even though we may not be guilty of many moral mistakes.

The balance between rules and goals is not easy to strike, and in the nature of the case we cannot give a rule that tells exactly how to do it. We learn by looking for examples of people whose passion for their goals seems appropriately limited by respect for the people and communities with whom they live, and whose respect for the rules seems in service of a larger purpose that grows from within them rather than being imposed on them from the outside. That is to say that we decide how well a person handles the balance between rules and goals by asking not just what goals the person has or what rules the person follows, but what kind of character that person has achieved. That is the next element of the moral life we want to examine in some detail.

CHAPTER 4

Virtues

We have to think about goals and rules together. Neither goals nor rules alone provide enough guidance for our choices to show us how to live a good life. But a good life seen as a whole seems to require something more even than goals and rules together. To have a good life we need goals to achieve and rules to follow, but we also need to understand who we are as persons. Our goals have to make sense in light of what we believe we ought to do, but both of those aspects of the moral life together must make sense in light of who we are and what we have done in the past. A student cannot say that her goal is to relieve human suffering by finding new ways to treat diseases if she has no head for biochemistry. A middle-aged man cannot plan a career of selfless service as a missionary if he has made commitments to a family, home, and business that are closer to hand. I cannot expect people to trust me as a wise person from whom to seek advice if I have consistently failed to keep my promises or lived my life in a way that others want to avoid, not emulate.

So alongside the goals we set and the rules we keep, an important part of a good life is the *narrative* in which we recount the things we have done and the choices we have made as well as the circumstances of our lives about which we had little or no choice.[1] Retelling our story explains to others and to ourselves how we have become the people for whom it makes sense to have the goals we have and to follow the rules we follow.

A narrative, of course, is not just a list of things that have happened. Forming a narrative is a creative act in which we lift some things up for special emphasis while others are set aside or forgotten. Moments that mark a decisive break with the past are important to a narrative, such as a change of career or a move to a different part of the country that separates us from family and the place where we were born. The points where we experience God's presence in our lives and commit ourselves to God in faith mark turning points in our narratives, conversions that enable us to face old challenges in new ways or move on to new tasks to which God is calling us. But our narratives are also composed of the stories of how God and other people have worked in our lives to lead us to those decisive moments, even if we did not see how that was working until many years later. Our narratives include dramatic events that change us, but also the routines of daily life that shape us. Our narratives recount the places to which we are tied and the people whom we have loved and from whom we have learned.

Forming a narrative is a creative act, but if it is to be useful for the moral life, it cannot be wholly the product of imagination. We all know people whose narratives include things they did not do and successes they only wish they had achieved. Even these fictions, of course, tell us something about the people they are, but we would want to include in a full account of their narrative the story of how they learned this tendency to exaggerate and why they have the need to do it. A narrative must be selective to be comprehensible, and it must be imaginative to put the emphasis in the right places; but it must also be truthful. It must tell a story about a person or a group that depicts them as they really are, not as they wish they were or as they want others to see them.

We sometimes daydream about how our lives would read if someone turned them into a book, or we may make a game of choosing the actors who would play the key roles if our lives were turned into a movie. But the fact is that we are all the time creating just such a narrative to help us deal with the choices we face now. If it is a truthful narrative, and not just a fantasy, it will help us to understand our own moral problems and those of others. That is why popular television programs and advice columns in the newspapers depend so heavily on telling people's stories. Without those narratives, any advice we give sounds trite and general, like a slogan on a bumper sticker or a sentimental wall plaque in a shopping mall gift shop. It is only when you know the person on whose wall you want that plaque to hang that the generalities embodied in proverbs and mottoes and slogans really become part of the moral life.

The narrative is more than a list of events. It is a story about how events made someone into a certain sort of person who faces today's choices in a particular way. Or a narrative may be the story of a group of people, even a whole nation. How could we understand the independence and individualism of the people of the United States without the narrative of the pioneers crossing the prairies in their covered wagons and staking out their farms in the wilderness? How could we appreciate the resilience and determined nationalism of the Russians without the story of their sufferings in the face of repeated foreign invasions?

Narrative helps us to understand character. We learn about people as individuals and as groups by learning their stories; when we know those stories well enough, we know something about the goals they will pursue and the rules they will follow as they face choices in the future. That is how narrative fits into our understanding of the moral life, whether the life in question is our own or that of others.

But if that is so, how can we make these narratives part of the study of ethics? We can formulate goals and rules, but it almost seems that we have to retell every story to get at what is really important in a moral discussion. That leaves us, in the end, with many stories, but perhaps not with so much clarity about choices.

The solution to this problem, tested over a very long time in the study of ethics, is to think about narratives in terms of *virtues*. Each character and each narrative is unique, and yet there are certain recurrent patterns that enable us to compare narratives and characters. Consider again that pioneer staking out a homestead in the wilderness. His story is very different from that of a Swiss townsman claiming freedom from a feudal overlord in the waning days of the Middle Ages, yet we recognize in each of them a quality of character that is developed in their experience and makes their actions possible—a quality of character that we call independence. It is the same quality that we recognize in English and American women in the nineteenth century who broke with conventional women's roles to become leaders in social reform movements or to take up professions that had been restricted to men. Different narratives from different times and places, yet we recognize a common trait of character that unites the people in these stories—at least in the way we tell these stories to ourselves.

Out of long experience and many stories, we create a vocabulary of personal characteristics that we recognize as part of the moral life and that we take into the understanding of our own moral lives. These characteristics we call virtues.

What Is a Virtue?

Virtues are the admirable qualities of persons that emerge from an examination of their narratives and that shape their moral lives. A system of thinking about ethics that centers on virtues is sometimes called an *areteology*, or an *areteological ethics*. The technical terminology here derives from *arete*, the word that Aristotle and other Greek philosophers used for virtue, just as deontological and teleological ethics take their names from the Greek words for "duty" and for "goal."

When we start thinking about virtues in the abstract, we are apt to start building lists of the qualities we admire in others or that we would like to see in ourselves; but it is important not to lose the connection between these admirable characteristics of persons and the narratives

63

through which we learn to identify them. We sometimes think of a list of virtues rather like a list of moral rules. Honesty, courage, and kindness become shorthand for "Don't lie," "Don't run away from problems," "Be attentive to the needs of others," and so on. Worse still, "virtue," in the way we often use the term, becomes reduced to following the rules of appropriate sexual conduct, so that someone—usually female—has her virtue as long as she follows these rules and loses it when she breaks them. When we limit the concept in these ways, the essential connection between a virtue and the characteristics of a person is lost.

So what is a virtue? How can we speak about virtue in ways that retain the richness and variety of our narratives while still helping us to come to a systematic understanding of the moral life?

An early answer that is still useful was supplied in Aristotle's *Nicomachean Ethics*. A virtue, Aristotle said, is a pattern of behavior learned through practice, so that it becomes part of the way a person normally tends to act. Having the virtue of kindness does not mean knowing intellectually how a kind person would act. The teacher of ethics has to have that intellectual knowledge, so that he or she can identify kind people and kind actions and point them out to the pupils. But people who have the virtue of kindness are people who have actually done acts of kindness to the point that they regularly do the kind thing. Aristotle thought about this as being very much like other kinds of practical learning. Indeed, the Greek word for virtue, *arete,* can be used for any sort of excellence, as the following passage suggests.

> The same causes and the same means that produce any excellence or virtue can also destroy it, and this is also true of every art. It is by playing the harp that men become both good and bad harpists. . . . The same holds true of the virtues: in our transactions with other men it is by action that some become just and others unjust, and it is by acting in the face of danger and by developing the habit of feeling fear or confidence that some become brave men and others cowards.[2]

Aristotle's way of thinking about virtue entered into Christian ethics many centuries later when Thomas Aquinas, the medieval theologian whose great "Summary of Theology" (*Summa theologiae*) has become one of the basic sources for Roman Catholic thought about theology and ethics, adopted the Aristotelian account of virtue as the starting point for his own thinking on the subject. Virtue, Aquinas said, is a *habitus,* the perfection of a human power in action.[3] The relationship to our English word *habit* is obvious, and our idea of a habit is a useful point of connection to what Aristotle and Aquinas had to say about virtues, provided that we are careful to avoid our more modern fixation on bad habits, which are usually acquired as a by-product of some sort of thoughtless behavior. A virtue is a habit in the sense that it is something that we do without thinking about it, though like most good habits, we may have had to think about it a lot to learn it.

People who are virtuous just seem to know how to act in the way the virtue requires. A kind person treats other people in ways that show she cares about them and thinks about their needs. She does not overwhelm them with kindness, so that they start to feel guilty about her sacrifices. She does not give them what she thinks they need, regardless of what they want or value for themselves. She does not call attention to her own kindness, so that she becomes the center of events. She simply attends to people's needs in ways that show that she understands what those needs are, that she believes they are important, and that she takes real satisfaction in doing what she can to meet them.

When a person has developed a virtue, it may be so much a part of the personality that we say that she is just naturally honest or that he is instinctively kind. Doubtless some people acquire virtues more easily than others, but we all acquire them by practice. The mature person's almost automatic kindness begins with the child's awkward attempt to help a parent; every virtue we recognize as part of someone's personality had to begin with actions that were observed, encouraged, and imitated.

What we learn in acquiring a virtue is not just to do something regularly, but to do it well. Kindness, patience, honesty, and other virtues require more than just not doing the wrong thing. We know how to identify most virtues by specifying the vices that are their opposites. Meanness, irritability, and deceitfulness are vices that contrast with kindness, patience, and honesty; but a kind person has to do more than just avoid being mean, and there is more to honesty than not telling lies. There is something about a virtuous action that is just right, that hits the mark, that fits what the situation requires in a way that orders to be kind, patient, or honest cannot specify.

Aristotle tried to give a systematic formulation to this aspect of virtue by saying that a virtuous action is one that finds the right middle point between two ways of doing the wrong thing in the situation, one that is excessive and one that is deficient.[4] Courage, thus, is a virtue that finds the middle point between the excessive readiness to rush into dangerous situations that we call recklessness, and the lack of ability to face challenges that we call timidity or cowardice. Patience finds the middle ground between a hot-tempered insistence on immediate action and a passive acceptance of anything that happens. Aristotle's system may appear a little bit too neat for the complexities of our actual experience of virtue, but it makes the important point that there are many ways to fail in the effort to act virtuously and only a very narrow range of action that will qualify as a truly virtuous choice. The person who has acquired a virtue may not be able to articulate the rule that guides his or her choices, but what appears to be an easy, "natural" action is the result of sound judgment acquired through long observation and much practice. The ease and appropriateness of the action are as much a part of the virtue as the specific qualities of kindness, patience, honesty, or courage that we identify with the virtue itself.

People who have acquired virtues are not just following rules. The rules have become part of their character, part of the persons they are. Their narratives help us to understand their choices and actions in ways that we could not learn by reading a list of the moral rules they believe in or by asking them to tell us what their goals are. People who have virtues are dependable. We can trust them to choose and act in the way that their virtues require. We can even use them as examples to help us and others understand exactly what a virtue is. Indeed, Aristotle suggests that virtuous behavior is so complex and so specific that there may be no other way to identify a virtue than to point to the people whose actions display it.

Which Virtues?

So far, we've spoken in general terms about what a virtue is; and we've used a variety of examples that many people would recognize as virtues if they saw them in the choices and actions of other people. Kindness, patience, courage, and honesty are included on many lists of virtues. So are generosity, care, loyalty, and faith. It might be a useful exercise to make a list of virtues that you think are most important and compare it to the lists that other people whose judgment you trust would make. You would probably find a great deal of agreement on the most important virtues. But the longer the lists become, the more specific you get about the ranking; and the more those you are consulting differ from your own experience, the more likely the lists are to vary. Kindness is a virtue that most of us would recognize, and many of us would place it high on the list of virtues. But what about patriotism, a specific kind of loyalty directed toward one's country? Is that a virtue, or not? Where does it stand on the list? Some authors have included on the list of important virtues a virtue called docility, an attitude of obedience toward one's superiors and a willingness to be instructed by those who know better than oneself. Is that a virtue? Or does it simply reflect the preference that those in authority are likely to have for those who let others do their thinking for them and accept their assignments without question?

The fact is that our ideas about virtue are notoriously limited by our place in history, our particular culture, and the social position we occupy. After twenty-three centuries Aristotle can still help us think systematically about virtue, and we recognize many of the virtues on his list; but some virtues that are important to him strike us as very strange indeed. His "magnanimous" or "great-souled" man, for example, moves slowly and deliberately, never hurries himself at the behest of others, always maintains control of himself and the situation, and knows how to hold his social inferiors at an appropriate distance.[5] We know people who fit this Aristotelian picture, but they strike us as arrogant, not virtuous. Our ideas about virtue are apt to share more with those who have been shaped by the Christian values of humility and service to others; but even there we are puzzled by those whose understanding of Christian demeanor is all solemnity and seriousness and has no place for joy, let alone humor or fun. Our ideas of virtue are tied to class and culture, so that some value an open, loving disposition that rushes to embrace friends and family and is quick to share tears and laughter with others, while others praise the restraint that does not impose its feelings on others and leaves them private space for their joy and grief.

For all the differences between human cultures and societies, it is plausible to think that there are at least a few universal moral rules, especially the basic prohibitions that forbid us to kill or injure an innocent person, to deceive another for our own purposes, and to deprive people of things that are recognized as belonging to them. It is far less likely that there are universal virtues, actions that every culture would acknowledge as "just right" in the way that we recognize when we see someone acting virtuously in a context that is familiar to us. Kindness, honesty, and hospitality might be good candidates for consideration as universal virtues; but even with these, what will count as honesty and hospitality can differ remarkably between cultures, as anyone can testify who has spent much time in foreign travel or married into a different ethnic group. Virtue seems to be that part of the moral life that depends most on the particular place and time where it is lived. People can come to agreement on basic moral rules, and business today depends on swift agreement on goals that transcend national and cultural boundaries. But learning to appreciate the virtues of those from quite different backgrounds comes more slowly and requires more practice. Acquiring virtues, and coming to an understanding of them, has to go on in a community where important agreements about virtue are already shared. We are likely to relearn virtue several times as we go through life—moving into new communities, becoming part of a new family, learning and changing vocations, and discovering our unique roles in the communities of love, faith, and work that we inhabit. Learning to choose and to act so that what we do is just right is a lifetime task. Our best guides will not be books of rules or lists of virtues, but the people around us who seem to have got it right already.

Moral Virtues

Nevertheless, we are not entirely on our own in this exploration. For all that our learning of virtue has to take place in a specific community located at a particular place in history and society, we are connected in important ways to others who have thought about virtue and tried to capture its meaning. Especially, we should expect to find guidance in learning how virtues have been lived and thought about in Christian history.

Perhaps the most important list of virtues in Christianity is the set of personal characteristics and actions that are identified in the Sermon on the Mount as leading to true happiness, the Beatitudes (Matt 5:1-12). When Jesus says, "Blessed are the poor in spirit . . . Blessed are the merciful . . . Blessed are the peacemakers," he identifies what are supposed to be characteristics of the people who have heard him and tried to follow his teaching. There is immediately the suggestion that these virtues are not for everybody in the comparison of those who follow Jesus to salt (Matt 5:13) or yeast (Matt 13:33), which work changes in the whole of things through their presence in small quantities. Indeed, the characteristics that mark the disciples as blessed, or virtuous, are not the sort of things that most people around them would be seeking. To be poor in spirit, to share mourning, to be meek, and to suffer persecution are hardly ways of acting that Aristotle's great-souled man would think get it just right. Nor would most of those in our society who value their personal security and emotional independence. The most important list of Christian virtues seems to put an emphasis on humility and service that contrasts sharply with the prevailing ideas of virtue in the society where those words first were spread, and in our own society too.

Other passages in the New Testament, however, acknowledge a closer connection between Christian behavior and the virtues that other people would recognize. First Peter 2:12 admonishes Christians to behave in ways that even the Gentiles can recognize as honorable, and the characteristics of the good Christian in the Pastoral Epistles do not differ very much from other bits of moral advice that were in common circulation early in the second century.

By the Middle Ages Christian theologians generally recognized an important overlap between the ideas of virtue that their society had inherited from Greece and Rome and the Christian virtues that they learned from the Scriptures and the traditions of the church. Some of those ancient leaders seemed to be genuinely admirable people, and Christians learned much that they needed to know about their varied roles in society from the examples of Aristotle, Cicero, Marcus Aurelius (121–180 CE), and other philosophers and rulers from the earlier pages of Western history. Just as the natural law provided a common core of moral rules that all people could recognize,[6] so also there were key moral virtues that seemed to be respected by wise people through the ages, setting a standard of conduct to which Christians, too, should aspire.

Four virtues were identified by both Christian and classical writers as of special importance: temperance, courage, prudence, and justice. These were called the *cardinal virtues*, drawing on a Latin word, *cardo*, which means "hinge." The moral life turns on these four virtues as a door turns on its hinges.

There are many different virtues that we can see in the lives of other people around us and learn by practice to live for ourselves. Different philosophers will offer different lists of virtues or rank them in different orders. Different callings and ways of life will require different virtues from those who live them. You could hardly expect the commander of a military troop to live his life by the same virtues that shape the life of a scholar in a monastery or a shopkeeper in the city. Even in the medieval Christian world, which offered far less diversity in ways of life and ways of thinking than our modern world does, theologians and teachers of ethics recognized that there is no one list of virtues that will do for absolutely everybody.

What makes the cardinal virtues important is that they are the virtues that people need to develop in order to live by whatever other virtues are important for them. Whether your life requires a merchant's boldness to strike a risky bargain or a teacher's patience with a slow and unresponsive pupil, you will not succeed if you timidly retreat whenever someone suggests that you are risking too much or wasting your time. Even the virtues that are most important for you are sometimes inappropriate. You cannot take every risk, even in a life where the ability to tolerate risk and take a chance on the future is essential. The teacher who is always patient with the agitated and rebellious as well as with the slow and discouraged soon loses the discipline that is essential to teaching in the first place. And whatever virtues seem to be most important to your life, you have to keep them in balance with other good characteristics that you seek to cultivate, just as you have to keep your life in harmony with the lives of others around you who are pursuing different virtues. The merchant or solider who practices only boldness and never patience is not likely to survive very long.

The idea of the cardinal virtues rests on the insight that we have to acquire some habits in the way we live out our virtues in order to have any virtue work over the long run. Those habits on which the other virtues turn are themselves virtues, learned by observation and gained in our lives by practice. The identification of just these four—temperance, courage, prudence, and justice—may seem somewhat arbitrary, but that is because our modern understanding of what these words mean has become rather narrow. Reviewing what these four cardinal virtues meant to the moral theologians who adapted them from ancient philosophers and earlier Christian writers will help explain why they regarded these virtues as particularly important to everyone's moral life.[7]

Temperance involves knowing what your physical and mental health requires and regulating your pursuit of your goals and the things you desire so that everything you do contributes to your long-term well-being. The things we enjoy we tend to carry to excess, whether that involves too much good food and drink or staying up too late to enjoy the company of our friends or a favorite entertainment. Temperance is about knowing our limits and enjoying each good thing in a way that enables us to enjoy other goods in the future, rather than undermining some of our goals by how we pursue others. The temperate person does not eat so much at dinner as to be unable to enjoy the conversation afterward nor stay up so late with the conversation as to be unable to stay awake on the job tomorrow nor work so hard at success on the job as to miss the opportunity for dinner and conversation in the first place.

In the United States today, of course, our first thoughts about what temperance means are usually shaped by the temperance movement of the nineteenth century. This was really a movement for abstinence from alcohol and sometimes from tobacco and other harmful drugs as well. We need to understand the effects of drugs and stimulants on our minds and bodies, and a temperate person might well decide to avoid some of these altogether. But the virtue of temperance is not achieved simply by avoiding things. Temperance is a matter of linking what you choose and what you refuse in a whole pattern of life that makes it possible for you to live a good life for yourself and, indeed, to contribute to the good lives of others. The temperance movement was built in large part on the understanding that alcohol consumption not only harmed those who drank to excess, but also undermined their families and made their neighborhoods unhealthy and unsafe for everyone.

The virtue of temperance cannot be reduced to specific commitments to abstinence, then. It is also more than a general commitment to healthy living, as though our contemporary fixation on the importance of diet and exercise could provide a comprehensive guide to temperate living. Temperance is as much about how we use our minds and form our spiritual lives as it is about how we care for our bodies. Accepting a new management theory as the complete solution for your business, adopting a philosophical theory without asking critical questions about it, or letting a new retreat experience or study program become the sole focus of your spiritual life are all intemperate choices. The temperate person knows how to change and grow and explore new possibilities. Enthusiasm for a book, trying a new experience, plunging into a new activity or a new relationship all help to keep us alive and renewed, mentally and physically. Temperance is a matter of knowing that while we are alive and open to God, who is larger than our own lives, the new thing is never the last word for us and where we have been is never someplace that we can completely leave behind. Temperate people participate fully in the opportunities and experiences that are available now, but in ways that keep them available for new experiences and for the needs of others in the future.

Courage is perhaps the most familiar of the cardinal virtues, but we recognize it in many forms. Courage can be dramatic, as when rescuers enter a burning building at risk to themselves or when unarmed protesters face down troops and tanks to secure freedom for themselves and others. We also see courage in people who face serious illness and death without losing their capacity to care about others or their concern for the future. We see it in people who go about their lives with dignity in the face of prejudice and discrimination and in those who steadily resist the threats of their persecutors, even when their resistance has little chance of success. We recognize courage in leaders who risk unpopularity to stand up for principles.

The virtue of courage is not the specific acts of daring or self-sacrifice that we admire, but the habit that shapes our choice to act courageously. In courage, perhaps, we see most readily how all of the moral virtues work. People who perform sudden feats of bravery often report that they did not think about what they were doing, and people whose courage endures in the face of long struggles with illness or persecution do not seem to become different people when they summon up the courage to resist the next challenge. Courageous action seems to flow almost automatically from these people. It is appropriate to who they are. Yet we know that not everyone reacts courageously in such situations. We try to discipline ourselves and to educate our children to face the smaller risks and disappointments of daily life so that when the time comes, we and they will be able to meet the more dramatic and dangerous challenges too. It takes courage for an awkward fourth grader to face the teasing of classmates or for an office worker to resist the petty humiliations imposed by an overbearing boss. We do not always take these displays of everyday courage seriously; but unless we learn and practice such disciplines, it is unlikely that we will be ready to respond

71

when the occasion calls for a sudden act of great risk or for steady endurance in the face of truly overwhelming dangers.

What makes courage a moral virtue is not just the quality of action, but also the worthiness of the goal. There is a long debate in moral philosophy over the question of whether a person can be courageous in the service of a bad cause. Answers to that question differ, but most writers agree that courage, as a virtue, requires a conviction that the purpose to be served by the courageous action is a good one. We may, sometimes grudgingly, recognize courage in our opponents, provided that we are convinced that they sincerely believe in their cause. By contrast, thieves who do great feats of daring to elude capture because they do not want to miss their chance to share in the loot probably should not be described as courageous, even though we feel some residual admiration for their nerve or get a little adrenaline rush of our own from watching their exploits at the movies.

What makes courage a cardinal virtue is that we cannot act on any of the virtues for very long without it. Even virtues such as patience and kindness, which seem to lead to actions quite different from the actions we associate with courage, require that we continue to be patient and kind in the face of opposition from others and loss to ourselves. Virtues will not come to much if we stop acting virtuously whenever we run into a problem. Courage enables us to put all of our other virtues at the service of the good we hope to do.

Prudence, like temperance, is tricky to understand in modern terms. We are apt to mistake it for merely being cautious and to wonder how we can make it into a virtue that stands without contradiction alongside courage. Yet it is clear that courage will quickly become mere recklessness without some thought about when it is appropriate to be courageous. Patience, likewise, may become procrastination if we are unable to determine when the time for waiting is past and the time for action has come. Generosity can be merely wasteful if our giving is not directed toward real needs in ways that show some prospect for solving the problem. Prudence is a habit of choosing actions that will make our other virtues effective. Without it our attempts to do good are likely to fail, and even worse, our failures are apt to make others think that trying to do good is slightly ridiculous in the first place. Failures of prudence tend to bring the moral life into disrepute.

Here again, we find ourselves thinking about patterns of choice and action that are not easily reduced to rules. We recognize the prudent person not because he or she has a rule that says, "Never exercise your generosity on a cause that you do not understand," but because we notice that this person asks questions before giving. The questions seem to be good ones and not just excuses to delay or avoid giving altogether. The prudent person seems to know when the information is enough and when there is a need to dig for more of it. A prudent person gives generously, but not blindly. A prudent person cares for people in need with kindness, but avoids making them dependent on the care of others. It is difficult to specify by the rules exactly what kindness requires and when it has become too much. That is where prudence comes in. We recognize in the examples set by others and learn through our own experience just what each of the moral virtues requires. Kindness that wastes resources and creates dependency is morally preferable to raw selfishness, but a prudent person knows how to be kind without doing unintended harm or leading people to question whether kindness is a good idea.

We need to learn prudence because the moral life is more than a series of bumbling attempts to do good. A measure of effectiveness is required if we are to be good people and not simply people who are full of good intentions. Virtue is never assured of success. If it were, we would not need courage. Prudence, however, makes success more likely by keeping our virtues connected to the possibilities and limits that are really a part of our present situation. Without prudence our virtues are apt to appear slightly old-fashioned, aimed at honoring a form of life that no longer exists by imitating how people lived in the past when they were trying to live good lives. Prudent people come to our attention because they have figured out how to live good lives now.

Justice, like prudence, is a habit of thinking about situations and choices in ways that make it more likely we will actually achieve the good things we intend when we make a moral choice. The distinction between prudence and justice is sometimes difficult to make; but we may say that, in general, prudence is about the effective pursuit of a particular good, while justice is about the appropriate choice of which goods and goals to pursue. Thus we say that a person is just when he chooses to spend money to help an old friend who has done him many favors to recover from the loss of a job, instead of using those funds to help a new acquaintance with medical bills after an accident. Both of those are good things to do, but the claims of old friendship and assistance in the past take priority. If you must make a choice of whom to help, the appropriate choice is to assist the one who has provided you with help in the past. The just person will choose to help an old friend in situations like this one. The prudent person, of course, will also render that assistance effectively, neither embarrassing his friend by doing so publicly nor making him feel dependent and reducing his ability to help himself.

Justice derives its meaning as a virtue of persons from its primary meaning as the appropriate distribution of things in a society or an institution. A society is just when the things that make it possible for people to have good lives are distributed fairly, so that people can believe both that their basic needs will be met and that the contributions they make to the whole society will be rewarded.[8] Additionally, a just society must assure that persons are treated fairly in transactions, so that they actually get what they bargain for, and must provide just punishments for those who violate the requirements of justice. Justice in society and in institutions thus has to do with systems to distribute goods appropriately among the people, and systems to restore justice when it is disrupted.

Justice as a virtue of persons has to do with the same sort of choices about goods, goals, and claims that a society must make when it decides about justice. The just person is one who can balance a wide variety of possible goods to choose the ones that are appropriate. The connection between the virtue of justice in persons and justice in society is most clear when the person must choose between goods that affect other people. It is a good thing, for example, to take care of oneself and to develop one's skills; but a person who invests large sums in exercise equipment and puts a high priority on tennis lessons while turning down the United Way appeal and foisting extra work off on colleagues in order to meet the personal trainer may be acting unjustly. A just person appropriately balances the claims of others and the needs of the self. As with other virtues, it is difficult to formulate a rule that would tell us in advance what the appropriate balance is.

Justice in choices that relate to other people requires, in the end, that we think comprehensively about the goods that we are pursuing as individuals. The balance between self and others has to be struck in each particular case; but unless those choices add up to a coherent plan of life for the person who is making them, any good that person may do is unlikely to continue for very long. Just people lead balanced lives, balanced between both their needs and the claims of their neighbors, and between the various good possibilities that make claims on their time, energy, and skill. A just person will have learned through experience to think carefully about the balance between different sorts of goods. We will recognize such people, as we do those who have learned the other moral virtues, by the fact that their choices seem right, even if we could not say in advance what those choices ought to be.

Theological Virtues

People who live good lives have good goals and follow moral rules, but many would say that we know them most readily by their virtues. Good habits of choice and action, guided especially by temperance, courage, prudence, and justice, shape good lives. A large number of the people who have written about ethics in Western traditions of philosophy and religion, from Aristotle's time to the present, have been able to agree on the importance of virtue, and of the four cardinal virtues in particular. Understandings of specific virtues differ greatly from place to place and time to time, but few have denied the importance of education that helps people to identify virtues and the actions associated with them. Few would doubt that practice in these virtues and actions is what makes us over the long run into people who have good lives and who would be recognized by their neighbors as good people.

Christians have participated in this broad agreement about how the moral life should be lived. As we saw, the early Christian emphasis on humility and care for others differed from the ideas about virtue that prevailed in non-Christian philosophy, and over time Christian ideas significantly changed the understanding of virtue in Western society. But Christians were largely able to adopt the ideas about how virtues are put into practice that they learned from reading Plato (428–348 BCE), Aristotle, Cicero, and other Greek and Roman authors.

Where Christians differed was in their understanding of how the moral life starts and how serious the obstacles to it are. People just do not seem to learn the habits of the moral life the same way they learn through experience to avoid hot stoves and to look both ways before crossing the street. They do not retain habits of virtue the same way they maintain the motor skills required to ride a bicycle or the habit of brushing their teeth every day. There seems to be something at work in our lives that keeps drawing us away from the habits of virtue and makes it difficult to act on them, even after we have learned to recognize what they require.

What stands between us and virtue is sin. Christians understand that sin is something much more serious than the simple fact that we often fail to do the things we know we ought to do. Sin is a fault at the center of human life that keeps us turned in upon ourselves, so that we cannot love God or live the good life as God intends for us to live it. There is no way to overcome this fault by ourselves because left to ourselves we do not want to overcome it. We cannot even recognize it as a fault. Looking out for yourself, we think, is just what normal people do.

The good news that Christians proclaim is that although we can never overcome sin by our own efforts, God has acted decisively to overcome it for us, turning us from ourselves to God and showing us, in Jesus, what life is like when it is lived in love for God and for other people.

Clearly, when we understand life in these terms, we cannot think of virtue exactly as Aristotle did. In addition to the moral virtues, there must be characteristic changes in human life that mark the turn from self to God; and these, if Christians have understood the matter rightly, must be God's gifts, not our achievements. In addition to those cardinal virtues that enable us to learn and maintain the other moral virtues, there must be *theological virtues,* habits of choice and action that guide us in seeing our lives in relation to God and help us to persevere in that orientation, even when it is not immediately supported by our experience or by the people around us.

For Christian writers like Thomas Aquinas, who sought to integrate what he had learned about the moral life from the philosophers' accounts of moral virtue with what he had learned from Christian theology about God's action to overcome sin, the theological virtues to be set alongside temperance, courage, prudence, and justice were conveniently summarized in the three abiding realities mentioned in 1 Corinthians 13: faith, hope, and love.

Like the cardinal virtues, the theological virtues of faith, hope, and love are "hinges" on which the good life turns. Without them all the other virtues we can acquire are unstable. Without faith, hope, and love, patience and kindness are apt to evaporate under stress or, worse, to be transformed into attempts to get one's own way under the pretext of consideration for others. Who has not experienced the dear, kind person whose generous acts always somehow manipulate us so that we end up serving the one who appears to serve us? To be turned in upon yourself so that even doing good is shrewdly calculated to your own advantage makes the moral life impossible from the start. Even a practiced cultivation of the cardinal virtues cannot prevent that. Temperance, courage, prudence, and justice make us more effective in the application of moral virtues; but this will not help us very much if our pursuit of goodness is directed, in the end, toward our own gain. What we need is a reorientation of our life so that relationship with God becomes central to what we are seeking and relationships with other people are not just instrumental to our own self-improvement.

This reorientation begins with faith because we must trust that there is a reality beyond ourselves in which our goals find fulfillment and where our efforts finally make a difference. Without that reality there is no point to worrying about anything except in terms of how it makes our own life better. Without faith the instrumental goodness that sees virtue as a highly refined form of personal success is the highest kind of goodness we can achieve.

The theological virtues require a fundamental reevaluation of our lives. If the moral virtues challenge the mistaken choices we have made and the wrong we have done, theological virtues challenge our ideas about our goodness. The smug satisfaction that we have done the best we can and that the rewards we have received are the least we deserve dissolves before the recognition that we have very effectively taken care of ourselves, even at those points where we were apparently most concerned for the welfare of others. Just for that reason the reorientation of life by faith also requires hope. Despair is the great risk of the religious life. Once we begin to measure our lives, not by the everyday standards of character and conduct, but by the orientation of self toward God that faith requires, any honest assessment of what we have been becomes very painful. Without hope that this burden of guilt can be lifted, it would be impossible to continue the reorientation of our lives that the theological virtues require of us.

Love, too, is a presupposition of life shaped by the theological virtues, as well as its goal. Even faith and hope can be self-centered if they amount to no more than the belief that there is a God who has the power to serve our interests better than we can do it for ourselves. Love is the orientation of individual life toward a center outside of itself, recognizing that my own value is not absolute, but derives from relationship to God. Love, likewise, values other people and things as they are related to God and not as they are useful or important to oneself. Love as a virtue, as a habit of choice and action, consistently does those things that enable others to flourish as persons with their own dignity and their own relationship to God. It may draw us very close to them in personal relationships or set them free to be themselves at a distance or even in opposition to us. But it never makes them subservient or dependent on us.

Such habits of choice and action cannot simply be learned through practice, as other human excellences are. We either have faith, hope, and love, or our efforts at the moral life will be limited to the instrumental goodness that a disciplined cultivation of the cardinal virtues makes possible. Christianity affirms that faith, hope, and love are gifts of God's grace. They are perhaps like other virtues in that we see our need of them when we observe the lives of others in whom these virtues are present and especially as we see faith, hope, and love embodied in the life of Jesus of Nazareth.[9] But they cannot be acquired by setting out to learn them. There is an enormous difference between saying to someone, even in the most encouraging and supportive way, "See that virtuous person over there. I want you to watch what they do until you can do it too," and saying, "You are loved. Now what are you going to do?" Faith, hope, and love must be cultivated in the second way. They can only be acquired in the confidence that they have already been given. "We love," says the epistle of John, "because he first loved us" (1 John 4:19).

Virtue in the Christian Life

In the history of Christian thought, the theological virtues of faith, hope, and love are often treated as the most important virtues and as the basis of the moral life for Christians. Because the theological virtues are God's gift, they are different from the moral virtues, which people can perfect by practice. The moral life as Aristotle understood it begins by observing those whose habits of choice and action seem to mark them as good people. We then learn to make our own judgments in the same way they do, avoiding both excess and deficiency and hitting the middle point that is the right choice.[10] There is nothing mysterious or at all religious about this. People simply make up their minds to become good people and apply themselves to the task. The picture in the New Testament, especially in Paul's writings and in the letters of John, is quite different. Here, only a fundamental redirection of life in relationship with God gives the virtues of faith, hope, and love through which a person can begin to deal with others in ways that we might recognize as virtuous.

The difference between the moral virtues and the theological virtues is so striking at this point that some Christian writers have wondered whether the moral virtues are really virtues at all if they seem to be found in people who do not also have the theological virtues. If, in the end, it is oneself that one loves and not God, does it make sense to call that person's generosity, honesty, or patience a virtue? If one's moral life really extends only to securing the best possible life for oneself, is the boldness and tenacity displayed in holding onto that life really courage? Augustine decided that even the highest moral achievements of the pagans could not really be called virtues.[11] Orientation of one's life toward God and God's purposes is so basic to the Christian moral life that it is sometimes difficult for Christians to imagine a truly moral life in which this element is absent.

Perhaps, however, this assertion that true virtue must be centered finally on God also runs the serious risk of becoming a self-centered claim that only we Christians deserve to be taken seriously in living the moral life. Living amid those who risked their lives to resist Nazi tyranny in Germany, Dietrich Bonhoeffer (1906–1945) observed that the evidence of genuine moral commitment and of costly self-sacrifice on behalf of others is very strong among some people who have no Christian commitments and even among some who actively reject the Christian faith.[12] Perhaps it is both unloving and unjust to disparage their virtues.

What is clear, from the writers of the New Testament to the theologians of the twentieth century, is that the Christian moral life begins as a response to God's gifts. The good we do springs not from fear of punishment or from a desire for the approval of other people, but from the love of God working in our lives.

That is not to say that being kind or patient, just, generous, or courageous comes to us easily or automatically. The theological virtues of faith, hope, and love do not make you a good person or give you a good life. You have to work at that in much the way that Aristotle first described it—observing, practicing, disciplining yourself in virtuous choices and actions until they become real habits with you. Thomas Aquinas, John Wesley (1703–91), and others spoke of this disciplined Christian living that comes after the initial reorientation of life toward God as *sanctification.* Just as they were quite certain that salvation is God's gift and not the result of our works, they were equally clear that this transformation of the habits of daily living into a genuine life of love toward others requires persistent, careful work on our part. In that, as in all of life's challenges, we have God's help, but we must also join in bringing the result to pass.[13]

Learning and sustaining the virtues that transform a Christian who has the gifts of faith, hope, and love into a person with a full moral life require self-knowledge and self-discipline. The tasks are sometimes lonely, but they are not accomplished alone. We live our faith in community with others, both in the community of faith that is the church and in the wider civic community. One of the most persistent questions of our time is whether these communities in which we live are the sorts of places that can support us in the effort to live a good life. Can our churches teach us virtue? What should we make of the tensions, conflicts, and divisions among Christians that often seem to bring out the worst in them, rather than enable them to live at their best? Can we expect assistance in living virtuously from the businesses, schools, and governments that shape most of our days, or must we actively resist the values they teach in order to live a good life? Those are the questions we will turn to in the next chapters.

CHAPTER 5

Church

No one can live a good life all alone. We depend on other people for material goods we need to survive each day, and our well-being is tied to the health and happiness of the people who are closest to us. Living a good life may begin as a self-centered effort—most of human life does—but we quickly find that the search for a good life involves us with other people who are affected by our choices and actions.

But our search for the good life involves other people as more than partners in meeting each other's needs. The people we live with become our teachers and coaches in ethics. We learn how to apply moral rules and what goals are really worth having from people who share our lives. They become our chief examples of virtue, and their encouragement helps us to live a good life.

Then there are people who teach us ethics by helping us to see new questions and showing us new possibilities for virtue. They may not be so directly involved in our lives as the first kind of teacher, but they break us out of our familiar ways and call into question ideas that we may never have examined. We may see them at first as threatening or evil or just different; but if we take the trouble to understand them, we come to see our own lives in a different light.

We need both kinds of people to learn how to live a good life. We need the support and encouragement of intimate friends and family who share our lives and whose goals, rules, and virtues are very much like our own. But we also need to encounter people who surprise us with their wisdom and kindness, though their lives are strange and even repugnant to us. We need to meet real members of groups we have known only in myths and stereotypes, both to learn about their real virtues and to call into question the ways we learned the myths and stereotypes.

For Christians, both kinds of moral learning happen in church. Our Christian communities are often the most important source of close friends and enduring support outside of our families. We trust the people with whom we worship, pray, and study because they share our values and commitments; and especially when those values are challenged, we seek support in a tight community whose members will reassure us that we are doing the right thing. Yet the church is also the main place where most of us meet people whose lives are very different from our own. Mission projects put us into contact with people who live in extremes of poverty and isolation, but who find the resources to share hospitality with us. Church gatherings allow us to meet people whose race or culture or sexual orientation would exclude them from the places where we spend the rest of our lives, and yet we find common ground in shared faith that overcomes the bitterness on both sides of old divisions.

These two ways of learning in the church are part of the moral lives of most Christians, yet they are often in tension with each other. The community of shared faith supports our beliefs and encourages us to distinguish ourselves from those who do not share our faith. This is the community of the narrow gate and the straight path, which few will find (Matt 7:13-14). The inclusive community of God, by contrast, calls us out of familiar places and expects to find God in new people and new ideas, even if those ideas challenge accepted beliefs. This is the community that believes God has other sheep in other folds, and that Jesus' prayer is that these diverse communities might find their way to unity (John 10:16).

Just how small and carefully defined our church must be or how wide and inclusive it may be, have been questions for the Christian community from the beginning. In the New Testament, and especially in the Acts of the Apostles, we see hints of tension within the original community of disciples. Some thought that their distinctive Jewish way of life, shaped by obedience to the law, should also be a part of the Christian calling. Other leaders, like Peter, saw that God's spirit was available to the Gentiles too (Acts 10:34-48). Paul became the historic voice for the mission to the whole world, Jews and Greeks alike, but his triumphant vision of a whole creation united in Christ occasionally finds expression in exasperation with those who seek to confine the new faith within the rigid forms of the old law (Gal 5:7-12).

Paul's community of faith is free from legalistic constraints and ethnic prejudices, uniting all who share faith in Jesus as the Christ. Yet even for him, there are boundaries. The faith expressed in personal experience and local communities must be recognizably connected to the faith of the original witnesses to Jesus' resurrection, and innovations that link it to esoteric beliefs or dubious moral practices are excluded (1 Cor 15:1-11; Rom 6:1-4).

Questions about the nature and boundaries of true Christian community have returned again and again in the history of the church. After Christianity became the common religion of people in Europe, the presumption grew that most people were in some sense Christian. They shared the beliefs of the church, even if they did not think very much about them, and they participated at least occasionally in its worship. Its ceremonies marked the high occasions of their lives—the births, marriages, and deaths. This assumption that there is a Christian community that includes everyone except those who explicitly exclude themselves from it persists in many places today, even though the diversity of people and the variety of Christian churches is much greater than it was in the age when the assumption was formed.

There are also, however, many examples of Christian groups organized around a strict understanding of the boundaries of their faith. Especially in the American context, where established churches disappeared early in the nineteenth century, Christians were free to organize themselves into congregations and denominations that shared distinctive views of the Bible, sacraments, and church order. Most of our denominations have lived with the same tension that strained the early church: They invite everyone to join their community of faith, and they also seek to define that community in ways that maintain a purity of faith and practice that leaves some on the outside.[1]

This is more than a source of controversy in the life of denominations and congregations. It is also a profound theological problem. How are we to understand a faith that we are called to share with the whole world when it seems that some people take hold of that faith in ways we cannot accept? For some, the answer is simply that those who understand Christianity differently are wrong. These Christians will be vigilant to expose error where they find it and active to remove those who teach it from the community. If we ask why these divisions arise in the life of the church, their answer may be that God uses error to test our loyalty to the true faith or that God uses us to keep others from falling under the influence of false doctrine. For these Christians, disagreements on matters of faith become points of clear choice between right and wrong, true and false, good and evil. Living a good life has to involve such choices, for we can hardly think that someone is living a good life if he or she is confused or mistaken about such important matters.

Other Christians say that these divisions are not occasions to decide who is right and who is wrong, but opportunities for reconciliation and reminders of our need for humility before God's purposes, which often exceed our understanding. Sometimes, indeed, the same Christian may express both approaches. Augustine was vigorous in his opposition to those his church regarded as heretics, and he sometimes suppressed them with brutal persecutions; yet he also warned those who think that they have the true faith against overconfidence, since only God knows who will eventually be found within the City of God.[2]

For Christians who pay attention to Augustine's warning, divisions within the church are less an occasion for deciding between right and wrong than a reminder that God's work among people is not yet complete. The unity of the church is not something that Christians can accomplish in the present by their own power. It is rather something for which they hope as part of the divine plan for the reconciliation of all things in God (Col 1:20). Until then, Christians should pray for an end to their divisions; but they must act with humility and restraint when it comes to dealing with those who disagree with them in matters of faith. For those who understand God's purposes this way, it is far more important for Christians to join together to serve those who suffer from illness, poverty, natural disasters, and the cruelty of other people than it is for them to spend their time and energy determining who has the right version of the faith they all claim to share.

Both broader and narrower understandings of the church have been articulated across the centuries, and theologians continue to debate the nature and limits of Christian unity. Meanwhile, each individual Christian faces similar questions in his or her own life of faith. The questions are unavoidable because the kind of community we believe the church to be is the kind of community that will shape our search for the good life. What kind of community will that be? Will we place the emphasis on certainty and security in shared beliefs? Or will we stress the importance of learning from others whose faith and life may not be like our own?

The answers vary widely, and each of us may give different answers at different times. But our answers fall into three general types.[3] Some think of the church as *ecumenical*—a unity of faith in which all Christians share, despite the many different forms the church takes and despite the deep divisions on questions of doctrine and practice that divide us into many different sects, denominations, and national churches. Some think of the church as *confessional*—a community that shares carefully defined beliefs to which everyone who enters must assent. Still others think of the church as *missional*—a movement that constantly seeks to expand the community of discipleship by calling new members to join this mission. Those who enter are tested more by what they do than by what they believe.

What follows should not be seen as a guide to choosing between these three types. No real church or denomination perfectly exemplifies any one of the types, and most of them include elements of all three. But the differences in emphasis are important, and we want to examine them more closely in this chapter.

The Ecumenical Church

For some Christians, the thing that distinguishes the church from all the other organizations to which they might belong and all the other loyalties they might hold is that the church seeks to encompass the whole human world. Christian faith unites people across differences of race, nation, and culture. It makes us one with those who lived centuries before us and with those who will follow us in the centuries after. We may be loyal to our country. We may be people who feel a lot of team spirit or company pride. Often people feel that same kind of loyalty for their particular place in the Christian community. We love our local congregation, and we cannot imagine worshiping regularly anyplace else. We cherish our identity as United Methodists or Baptists or Presbyterians. But we know that all of those allegiances, including our loyalty to our church, are limited. Being part of the people of God is something else again. That connects us with a community that has no boundaries and that is not tied to a particular nation, place, or time. It is a universal or *ecumenical*[4] community.

For some Christians, this universality is key to how they understand the community in which they worship week by week. The churches that grew up in the early centuries of Christian history often reflected very closely the culture of the regions in which they were formed. Yet these Greek, Syrian, Armenian, and Coptic (Egyptian) Christians did not think of their church as Christianity for Greeks, Syrians, Armenians, or Egyptians, but as the Christian faith for the whole world. Today, churches from most of these traditions can be found in any large North American city, and they usually retain strong ties to the ethnic communities in which they originated. Though religion and ethnic culture are closely entwined, the mission of the church is not to preserve the culture, but to continue a witness to the faith as it was received. So Eastern Orthodox churches unite many different national and ethnic churches into a communion that shares forms of worship and theology derived from their ancient roots in the Greek-speaking part of the Roman Empire. They acknowledge the bishop of Constantinople as the "Ecumenical Patriarch," the head of a body of Christians that continues the witness of the apostles throughout the entire world.

In a similar way a worldwide church grew from specific local origins at the western center of the empire, in Rome. The pope, who is Rome's bishop, the successor to the apostle Peter, speaks to the whole world not simply as head of the organization that is the Roman Catholic Church, but as the voice of the apostolic tradition. For most North Americans, the word *catholic* probably just names another denomination—like the

Baptists, Episcopalians, and Methodists—but the name makes a stronger claim than that. "Catholic," like "ecumenical," recalls an ancient word for "universal,"[5] a church that sought to be not one among many, but the witness to the one faith for the whole world.

Problems begin, of course, when two or more universal churches find themselves occupying the same territory. Since the Great Schism, which divided Rome from the Eastern churches in 1054 CE, Christian history has been marked by excommunications, condemnations, and exclusions, but also by an underlying desire for unity that refuses to accept the idea of a permanently divided Christianity.

Most Protestant churches understood the particularity of their history more clearly from the beginning. Lutheran, Reformed, and Anglican churches originated just about the time that modern states were also forming in Western Europe; and the Protestant Reformation never achieved the comprehensive organization that the Roman Catholic church had spread across Europe during the late Middle Ages. Protestant churches became more clearly German, English, Swiss, or Swedish. They often existed alongside a continuing Roman Catholic presence, even in countries where the majority of the population adopted Protestantism. They experienced further divisions as Baptist, Quaker, Methodist, and pietist movements separated themselves from the already distinct Protestant churches. And when this array of Protestant churches moved with the European migration to North America and other parts of the world, they often found themselves next door to other Protestants who shared an even more bewildering array of histories, beliefs, and practices.

Yet even among the Protestants, the aspiration for universality did not disappear. Protestants could hardly find it in their history, but they could claim it as a hope. While the early centuries of Protestantism were marked by sharp divisions over ever finer points of doctrine, Protestants began to realize during the nineteenth century that alongside their theological divisions, they shared a common hope that all people could be united in the Christian faith. From this began the modern ecumenical movement, which stresses the unity of Christian churches, rather than their divisions, and works to overcome the theological and organizational barriers that separate groups of Christians from full participation in a common Christian life.

The early ecumenical movement was no doubt distinctly Protestant in its emphasis on structure and program and on the reunion of denominations that share a common heritage into a single organized church. Paradoxically, the effort to be universal in this way was necessarily confined to those Protestant churches that did not make large claims for their own universality, and it focused the most attention on denominational mergers between two or three groups that already had a lot in common. Efforts toward denominational union continue, but attention in recent years has shifted to dialogues that aim to increase mutual understanding and arrive at agreements that allow real sharing in specific acts of worship and specific forms of ministry. In recent decades these dialogues have come to include Roman Catholic and Eastern Orthodox representatives along with the Protestant participants.

When Christians express the ecumenical side of their faith, their minds are stretched and their faith is strengthened by knowledge of how other Christians live and pray. Some Protestant denominations have historically rejected liturgical worship, preferring the freedom of extemporaneous prayer to the regularity and order of ritual. Preachers and teachers have inveighed against the vestments, the liturgies, the rich colors, and the carefully repeated actions of Roman Catholic, Lutheran, and Anglican worship as little better than idolatry. Yet today many Protestants find their worship more meaningful when it adopts some of these liturgical forms. Albs and colorful stoles replace the traditional black robes of the pastors, the communion table displaces the pulpit at the center of the worship space, and the celebration of Holy Communion becomes a monthly, or even weekly, event. Meanwhile, Roman Catholics sing praise choruses and abandon the traditional anonymity of the confessional for services of penance that adopt some of the face-to-face examination of life in the presence of one's brothers and sisters in faith that has characterized Protestant prayer circles. It is not so much that all Christian worship is becoming alike as it is that its diversity can no longer be predicted by denominational labels.

The reach toward other forms of Christian life and understanding takes on global dimensions. North American United Methodists sit baffled through the mysteries of a Roman Catholic mass in a seventeenth-century church in Peru, until the congregation takes up a Spanish hymn that the Methodists have sung from their own hymnals at home. Volunteers in mission travel to Russia intending to share their living Christianity with people who have been stifled by seventy years of enforced atheism, only to find themselves awed by a Russian Orthodox spirituality that has endured through centuries of hardship. Christians from all denominations in Europe and North America find themselves learning from their counterparts in Asia, Africa, and Latin America, where churches are growing rapidly and taking on new forms that are less dependent on European cultural roots.

In practical terms, the reach toward other forms of spiritual life and other ways of understanding our relationship to God often extends beyond the bounds of Christianity to touch other religious traditions as well. Church agencies and official dialogues usually take care to distinguish "ecumenical" activities, which unite different branches of the Christian family, from "interfaith" events, in which Christians share with adherents of other religions. The popular understanding of "ecumenical," however, is more loosely defined. Suburban neighborhoods that once mingled Baptists, Presbyterians, Methodists, and Roman Catholics now include Jews, Hindus, Muslims, and Buddhists from a variety of ethnic and national backgrounds. Christians who genuinely care about their neighbors seek to understand all of them, welcoming the first Sikhs on the block with perhaps less suspicion than their grandparents greeted the first Roman Catholics.

Christians from non-European backgrounds, moreover, are beginning to recover spirituality, stories, and values from their ancestors. The first generations of converts discarded these things in a sharp break with their pre-Christian past, often enforced by the zeal of the European missionaries who were their teachers. Today, Native American Christians find in their tribal traditions a connection with the earth and a sense of their own identity that enriches their reverence for God's creation and their awareness of themselves as God's children. Asian and African Christians have become more adept at identifying the pre-Christian European elements in the missionary Christianity they first received, and they feel a new freedom to replace Christmas trees and wedding rings with symbols from their own cultural heritages.

An ecumenical perspective on Christian faith allows us to respect other people, despite differences in theology. It enables us to appreciate different forms of prayer and worship, whether or not they speak to us personally, and it opens us to learn even from those with whom we may continue to disagree. Ecumenical Christians find their faith strengthened by the discovery and exploration of other forms of Christian faith, and they regard the persistence of these differences as part of the mystery of God's purposes in history rather than as an occasion to make judgments about the faith of others.

The Confessional Church

A very different understanding of the church developed during the Protestant Reformation in the sixteenth century. Rejecting Roman Catholic claims to be the ecumenical Christian community, some Reformers emphasized instead the unity that comes from a shared understanding of Christian faith. What marks the true church is not that it extends through the whole world, but that it agrees on basic truths. The true church, indeed, may be quite small, compared to the large number of those who claim to be Christians. However, the true church is not identified by taking a poll, but by examining the beliefs of those who claim a place in it.

Of course, it would not be easy to hold such a church together if each person had to arrive at his or her own formulation of true Christian belief. The possibilities for argument among the intellectual elite would in that case be almost endless, while many other faithful people would be excluded altogether, not by the weakness of their faith, but by insufficient verbal skills. The key to creating this kind of church and holding it together, then, has been the writing of *confessions,* statements of faith that express agreement on basic theological points, such as the nature of God, the person and work of Christ, the effects of grace, and the practice of Christian worship. The century of the Reformation saw many such confessions, written or presented in large assemblies of preachers and scholars. Melanchthon (1497–1560) summarized Luther's (1483–1546) teachings in the Augsburg Confession of 1530. The Swiss Reformer Bullinger (1504–75) compiled the First Helvetic Confession in 1536, then in 1566 wrote the Second Helvetic Confession, combining Calvin's (1509–64) and Zwingli's (1484–1531) theology; and the Westminster Confession of 1646 summarized the faith of the English Reformation.

Confessions serve as statements of faith to which individuals can give assent. If the confession summarizes true Christianity, then those who accept it become part of the true church, and the true church is identified by its acceptance of the confession. The point, however, is not a thoughtless repetition of the words, but a genuine understanding of the points at issue. Hence the churches that adopted confessions of faith often at the same time wrote catechisms that provided their adherents with instruction, in question and answer form, regarding the key points of the confession. Although many of these churches retained the practice of infant baptism, they increasingly stressed an adult understanding and acceptance of the confession as the condition for full participation in the Christian community. Especially under the influence of the Awakenings, spiritual revivals that swept Britain and the British colonies in North America during the early 1700s, this adult entry into the church might be accompanied by powerful individual experiences of conversion and transformation; but for the confessional churches it was not the conversion experience, but the acceptance of the confession that marked one as a true Christian.

The writing of these summaries of doctrine did not end with the Reformation era. The Church of England adopted the Thirty-nine Articles of Religion in 1571. These articles were not, perhaps, so central to teaching and profession of faith as the confessions and catechisms of the Reformation churches, but they did provide a convenient summary of the distinctions between Anglican beliefs and practices and those of other churches, especially the Roman Catholics. John Wesley adapted these Articles for the use of American Methodists in 1783, and they have continued to serve as a standard for United Methodist teaching and preaching. In more recent times the United Presbyterian Church produced a comprehensive confession of faith known simply as the Confession of 1967. Unlike earlier confessions, which tended to emphasize the differences between the church making the confession and other religious groups, the Confession of 1967 stressed the centrality of reconciliation in Christian faith and life and sought a confession that would witness to Christian unity and overcome the sharp divisions that were apparent in American society at the end of the 1960s.

The growth in the number of confessions over the centuries and improved relations between Christian communions has reduced the emphasis on confessions as points of controversy. They have largely become a part of the heritage of denominations and of the Christian faith more generally. United Methodists include a number of these confessional documents at the beginning of their *Book of Discipline.* Lutherans give particular authority to the material included in the *Book of Concord,* a collection of confessions and catechisms first published in 1580 to help give unity to the Lutheran Reformation toward the end of its initial period of rapid expansion. Presbyterians recognize the official compilation of the *Book of Confessions,* which includes several of the more modern affirmations, like the Confession of 1967.[6]

Nevertheless, confessions remain very important, both for those churches that are historically identified as confessional churches, requiring their members to assent to one or more of the historic confessions, and for other Christian denominations and groups that have found the idea of a Christian confession a significant way to identify themselves in opposition to trends and forces in the religious and social life of their times. The idea of a confessional church may have originated with the Reformation, but it retains considerable power in church life today.

Probably the most important example in twentieth-century Christianity is the Confessing Church, which formed in opposition to the allegiance that many German Christians gave to Adolf Hitler at the beginning of the Nazi era. Insisting that Christians had to distinguish their loyalty as patriotic Germans from their worship of God, the Confessing Church claimed to be the true representative of the Protestant faith in Germany, basing its proclamation on the historic confessions that bound the Reformation churches together and rejecting the identifications of piety and patriotism that the Nazis were encouraging in the churches.

The Confessing Church did more, however, than affirm the historic confessions. It drew up its own declaration of faith at a synod meeting in the town of Barmen in 1934. The Barmen Declaration begins with this ringing affirmation of the exclusive loyalty of Christians to the saving message of Jesus Christ, as opposed to the secular salvation that was being proclaimed in the name of the Nazi ideology:

> Jesus Christ, as he is attested for us in Holy Scripture is the one Word of God which we have to hear and which we have to trust and obey in life and in death. We reject the false doctrine, as though the Church could and would have to acknowledge as a source of its proclamation, apart from and beside this one Word of God, still other events and powers, figures and truths, as God's revelation.[7]

On the strength of this affirmation, the Confessing Church set up a network of church leaders and made provision to train seminarians who would uphold its standards in the face of popular pressure for the Nazi alternatives. Some of the leaders of the Confessing Church, including Karl Barth (1886–1968), were forced to flee Germany soon after the synod at Barmen, but others maintained a strong network of Confessing Churches even after the beginning of the Second World War in 1939. Dietrich Bonhoeffer, well known for his participation in the resistance movement, which cost him his life just before the end of the war, served as a leader of the Confessing Church and wrote one of his most important theological reflections about the life of a Confessing Church seminary.[8]

The Confessing Church in Germany has provided an important starting point for theologians in other parts of the world who have had to define the requirements of faith against the expectations of their culture and to protect the church from becoming a mere instrument of other powers. In this twentieth-century context, the point of confession is not so much to define each detail of Christian faith against other possible interpretations. Those who initiated the Confessing Church in Germany were, in fact, among the most active members of the ecumenical movement. They wanted agreement with other Christians on matters of faith, not separation from them. But they also believed that it is necessary at certain points in history to define key Christian beliefs that cannot be compromised when the government and other powerful forces in the culture demand that the churches support their political and social aims. At that point a *status confessionis* exists, a situation in which the contrast between faith and culture is so great that the usual efforts to explain, interpret, and understand cannot continue. The church has no choice but to proclaim its faith in clear terms and set itself in opposition to the powerful forces that will demand its submission.

A *status confessionis* is not to be confused with the normal situation in most of our churches, which always struggle to maintain a balance between responsible participation in social life and sustained religious concern for society's failures and shortcomings. It is possible for most of us to be loyal citizens, even if, for example, we do not believe that the government's welfare policies measure up to the requirements of Christian compassion. We continue to try to be good participants in our local communities, even if we think that state and local leaders have made a mistake by developing the gaming industry as an important new revenue source. A *status confessionis* demands a different response. Those who believe that circumstances call them to confession must warn the government that no cooperation can be expected with policies that pose a direct challenge to Christian faith, and that they must warn other Christians that to go along with those policies will separate those who follow them from the historic community of Christian faith.

Few challenges rise to this level. Before the end of apartheid in South Africa, Reformed theologians debated whether the government's policies of racial isolation and exclusion posed a challenge to Christian faith that created a *status confessionis.* When the cold war confrontation between the United States and the Soviet Union led to the buildup of massive nuclear arsenals that could threaten all life on the planet, some argued that the military doctrine of mutually assured destruction created a *status confessionis* that demanded Christian rejection of the policy of nuclear deterrence.

More recently, social policies that permit abortion and cultural shifts within the churches that lead to increasing acceptance of gay and lesbian persons have prompted some to consider proclaiming a *status confessionis.* Calls are heard in the confessional churches for a reaffirmation of the historic standards and a withdrawal from ecumenical commitments that put these churches in partnership with others that are more accepting of these cultural changes. In The United Methodist Church, which has historically given less attention to confessions of faith than to practical activity in mission, a Confessing Movement has emerged, seeking to make use of the idea of confession to define the boundaries of the church more sharply for today.

Theologian William J. Abraham articulates the idea of a confessing movement today, which calls Christians to lift up their allegiance to Jesus Christ as Lord in distinction to all other loyalties and values, both outside and within the church.

> This confession is seen not only as central to the faith down through the ages, but as precisely that element in the faith which at this moment in history needs to be resolutely reasserted and reappropriated. Such a confession calls for the repudiation of christological alternatives that are sub-

Christian or post-Christian in nature; and it requires a positive embrace of the teaching of the church's Savior and Lord as an alternative to the moral commitments of the culture. Saying "yes" to Jesus Christ as Son of God, Savior, and Lord requires that we say "no" to other values, principles, and commitments that have been embraced as final and ultimate in the church and the culture.[9]

Here, as in the Barmen Declaration, the confessional affirmation of Jesus Christ as Lord and Savior implies an equally forceful rejection of all cultural realities and forces that would set themselves up as lord in place of Christ. This is true whether the cultural power is a definite movement that makes explicit claims to authority over all of life, as the Nazis did in the 1930s and 1940s in Germany, or whether the cultural power is the more diffuse understandings widely shared in American popular culture in the 1990s. It is characteristic of confessional movements in the twentieth century that their affirmations are directed not so much against divergent systems of Christian belief as against cultural norms that deny basic Christian understandings about the human person in relation to God. The religious dimension of the cultural conflict arises precisely because the cultural values that a confessing church must oppose often cloak themselves in religious language and symbols. The Barmen Declaration was directed against National Socialism as a political ideology, but also against the religion of the German Christians who clothed Hitler's politics with the biblical language of election and redemption. If contemporary confessing movements sometimes dismiss alternative positions with an abruptness that precludes serious theological discussion, that is in part because they are convinced that the roots of these positions are not theological at all, but represent a confusion of Christian beliefs with widely held secular ideas.

The power of a confessional church is its power to free the faithful from mistaken beliefs that are so generally held that they cannot be challenged in the institutions of the wider culture. In a time when most North American Christians are so comfortable with their situation and their society that they simply assume that whatever they believe is the Christian faith, it is important sometimes to start with the affirmation that Jesus Christ is Lord and ask what that would imply for all of the greater and lesser powers to which we offer daily reverence. The gospel has always been a demanding word for those who have many possessions and strong attachments (Luke 14:25-33). It may require the penetrating simplicity of a confessional faith to make that demand heard in an environment that offers elaborate rationalizations for its sanctification of wealth and security.

New problems may arise, however, if the confession itself becomes captive to the values of a specific culture or group within a society. The affirmation that Jesus Christ is Lord can free us from the fears that hold us captive to other people's prejudices and their exploitative plans for us; but that affirmation can also become a defensive, fearful assertion that my values and my way of life are Jesus' choices and that I will hear no questions about them. If Christian confession alone has the power to free us from the illusions that our society receives as truth, our situation will indeed be hopeless if some of those societal illusions become for us the content of the confession.

The Missional Church

A third way of understanding the church focuses on mission, on the activities by which Christians, working together, live out their faith in the world. A missional church has a vivid awareness of the differences between what people actually believe and how they act and the faith and life to which God calls them. People worship false gods, sometimes in religions that bind them to fear and superstition and sometimes— perhaps more often in the modern world—in their commitments to goals and values that lead them either to exploit their neighbors or to surrender themselves to exploitation by others. Women live in abusive relationships because they believe their suffering is God's will. Victims of injustice are told that their oppressors hold power by God's command. People follow religious precepts or moral commands that do not improve their lives or bring them closer to God, but render them stern and unforgiving, both toward themselves and toward others.

These people need to hear good news that effects a change in how they relate to God and to other people. If an ecumenical church sees the variety of God's work in the many different ways that people live their faith, the missional church sees first what is false and distorted and in need of correction. But unlike the confessional church, which begins the correction by setting the terms of faith straight, saying clearly what is and is not to be believed, a missional church calls for action. Lives must be changed, and the work of the church begins in action that makes those changes possible.

The action takes many forms. One of the most important is the proclamation of faith in Jesus Christ against the many other faiths that compete for our attention or hold us captive to their limited purposes. A missional church begins by calling people to abandon their idols and put their faith in the God made known in Jesus. A whole host of other changes follow from this first one.

But a missional church may call for many other kinds of action too.

Injustice that exploits people and puts their lives and labor at the service of masters they did not choose calls out for change, no less than the choice to serve false values and limited goals with a devotion they do not deserve. When a missional church takes action against injustice, this is also a way of proclaiming faith in God and the kinds of relationship between persons that true faith requires. In other cases missional churches are less concerned with large issues of faith and justice and more attentive to the needs and problems that keep individuals from living full and satisfying lives. From the beginning Christians have understood that physical pain, desperate poverty, or tormenting fears can keep people from God; and action to relieve these conditions for individuals where we find them has been part of how the church understands its mission.

Missional churches vary significantly in the kinds of action they embrace and emphasize. Advocates of one kind of mission sometimes criticize the priorities set by others, so that those whose idea of mission centers on proclamation may complain that a ministry that feeds the hungry or provides services for the poor does not do enough to bring the poor and hungry to faith in Jesus Christ. Those whose mission focuses on social justice may counter that it is hypocritical for Christians to claim that they care about people's souls when the church has such great resources and yet does nothing to relieve the basic physical needs of the people just outside its doors. Still others will respond that faith means nothing apart from changed lives, so that the real task of the missional church is to provide a framework of faith and discipline in which people can reclaim lives that have been shattered by addictions, abuse, and irresponsibility.

Listening to those arguments, which can be both loud and long lasting, dividing congregations and denominations, it is easy to forget the common idea that underlies all versions of the missional church. Whether the attention is centered on the truth of our faith, the justice of our society, or the integrity of our personal lives, the missional church proclaims the judgment that falls when our faith, our lives, and our understanding of justice are measured against the biblical standard. Our faith lacks the complete trust in God that Jesus taught in his parables. Our efforts to live a moral life are clouded in self-righteousness and hypocritical judgments that impose a severe standard on others and an easy one on ourselves. Our idea of justice focuses too much on secure possession of what belongs to us individually and pays too little attention to the human needs we all share and the stewardship of the earth for which we are all responsible.

The missional church proclaims judgment, but also calls for transformation. Like the ecumenical church, which understands that unity lies finally in God's hands, the missional church knows that the transformation of persons and societies is God's work. It proceeds on a timetable we do not control, and we do not always understand why it does or does not happen. Nevertheless, the missional church puts its emphasis on actions that aim at transformation. The gap between the way people actually live and the life to which the Bible calls them can be narrowed, and it is the task of the missional church to work with God to bring that about.

The emphasis on action and transformation leads to two questions that any missional church must answer carefully. First, what are the steps that lead from the biblical expectation to choices about present action? The year of jubilee (Lev 25:23-24), Isaiah's call for a faith that cares for the poor (Isa 58:6-12), and Jesus' blessing of the peacemakers (Matt 5:9) all call our ordinary ways of thinking and living into question, but what they imply for present action is not immediately obvious.

Determining how our lives and our society should be transformed is a complex process that involves both deep reflection on the meaning of the biblical standard and careful study of human nature and social reality as we find them in the world today. Returning the land to its original own-ers every fifty years, as the law of the jubilee requires, surely is not a practical system of justice today. (It is quite possible that it never really happened in ancient Israel.) But we can reflect on what the jubilee implies about how to limit the gap between the rich and the poor in a just society and what it would mean to organize our systems of law and justice so that people are both free to make their own choices and secure from the loss of basic resources they need to make a fresh start when those choices go wrong. Then, when we think we have figured out what the biblical standard requires, we have to check that against what social science tells us about how the economy works and the way people really make their choices so that we can be sure that our understanding of the Bible does not commit us to actions that in fact will inevitably fail. Those discussions can go on for some time as a church decides what to do about poverty or how to work for world peace or what sort of ministry to offer to those whose lives have been damaged by addiction. Indeed, the discussions should never reach a final conclusion because each action that a missional church takes will reveal new things, both about the bibli-cal message and about contemporary reality. What the missional church must avoid are the simple solutions that turn the Bible into a slogan or that too quickly identify biblical justice with some contemporary pro-gram. The missional church makes a commitment to transformative action, but also a commitment to continual reflection on how its biblical faith leads to the particular transformative actions it undertakes.

The second question that a missional church must answer concerns the scope of the transformations it expects. How far reaching are its goals? And who, exactly, is to be transformed? Only those to whom the message is proclaimed? Or perhaps also those who are doing the proclaiming?

A century ago, perhaps, a missional church would have found these questions easier to answer. The missionary expansion of the Christianity, especially Protestant Christianity, during the nineteenth century paralleled the spread of European and American technology and commerce across the globe. It was easy for missionaries and those who supported them to believe that other religions, even other forms of Christianity, would simply disappear as opposition from backward leaders ceased and the true faith became more widely known. Early in the twentieth century the Social Gospel movement envisioned a similarly complete transformation of religious and economic life in the United States.

> Individually we are not more gifted than our grandfathers, but collectively we have wrought out more epoch-making discoveries and inventions in one century than the whole race in the untold centuries that have gone before. If the twentieth century could do for us in the control of social forces what the nineteenth did for us in the control of natural forces, our grandchildren would live in a society that would be justified in regarding our present social life as semi-barbarous.[10]

What went unspoken in these hopeful visions of missionary expansion and social transformation was the presumption that in those who had the visions, the necessary transformations were already largely complete. There was no reason to study other religions or other cultures, except to learn how to tell them the truth that we already had fully in hand. We could state the requirements of justice with confidence that our version of justice had already been purified of the taint of self-interest by our careful attention to the biblical requirements. In short, the distance between the work of transformation in which we were involved and the new creation God had planned was not great.

More than a century of experience has made the missional church's understanding of the transformation it seeks more realistic. (We will give more attention in the next chapter to this realism about the church's role in society and how it developed.) That is not to say that the commitment to mission is any less. Indeed, it seems that people in the church today are likely to know more about its mission in other parts of their own country and their own city than their parents and grandparents did; they certainly have more opportunity for firsthand participation in the global mission than did those earlier generations who confidently expected the early triumph of Protestant Christianity over all other forms of faith.

Wherever we look, it is not hard to find people taking up those opportunities. Volunteers build houses in the inner city or turn their underused church gymnasiums into shelters for the homeless. Youth groups repair homes in the hollows of Appalachia or spread out to witness to their faith in suburban parking lots and on city street corners. Health professionals and educators join teams to provide basic medical care and literacy training, sometimes half a world away and sometimes just a few miles from their own homes and churches. The growth of missional activity that involves ordinary Christian people, members of typical congregations, is one of the most important stories in the life of the church at the end of the twentieth century; and what they learn from those experiences is likely to change our understanding of the missional church.

What participants in these experiences most often report is the discovery that they receive a great deal from the people they were sent to serve. Initially, some are overwhelmed by how difficult and different life is in these strange settings; but gradually, sharing homes and lives and labor with the poor gives them a new appreciation for the hospitality of those who have little in the way of material goods to share. They learn wisdom and patience from people who have lived hard lives with little opportunity for formal education, and they discover what trust and hope mean when they see these qualities in people who lack the security that those whose lives are more comfortable can take for granted. In short, the participants in today's missional church find God at work in places where they expected God to be absent. They see God in people whose faith may be quite different from their own or who may say they have no faith at all.

Participation in mission challenges their presuppositions and expectations, but it does not weaken their faith. Indeed, what they report is that their faith becomes stronger. Removed from the support of familiar surroundings where everyone shares a similar way of life and similar values, they see more clearly what they truly believe and trust.

What comes in for the most serious questioning is, in fact, neither the place where they are in mission nor the faith they bring to that task, but the old, familiar setting from which they came. Participants in today's missional church do not share the assumption of their nineteenth-century counterparts that learning and service all move in one direction, from the church to the mission. Because the missional church itself falls short of the biblical idea of faith and justice, participation in mission clarifies the understanding of what faith requires and helps to distinguish core Christian commitments from cultural prejudices and unquestioned assumptions. This should not be a matter of simply exchanging one set of prejudices for another. What is learned in mission must be examined, questioned, and prudently applied to new situations. But working in mission can spark new ways of thinking about people and their problems, both for the missional churches and for the individuals who participate in mission.

The effects of that new thinking are often most apparent when the one who goes on mission returns home. A week's work roofing houses, digging wells, or dispensing medicines makes a difference; but those results are not usually very dramatic when measured against the need. The biggest changes may follow from the different way that people see their families, jobs, and communities after that experience.

What Kind of Church?

The differences between ecumenical, confessional, and missional churches are real. There are denominations whose history links them more closely to one understanding or another. There are congregations that develop an ecumenical, confessional, or missional identity that attracts some people to them and leaves others cold.

In the Christian search for the good life, each kind of church has its place. Some who waver between faith and unfaith and are easily attracted to the false promises of secular prophets will seek the definitive word of a confessional church. Others who are easily drawn into disputes about words, but find it hard to put their faith into action will want the opportunities that a missional church provides. Still others whose world is expanding through education, business contacts, travel, and personal relationships will need the more inclusive vision of an ecumenical church.

The choices, however, belong primarily to individuals seeking a Christian community that will support and challenge the particular understanding of the good life that shapes their own belief and action. A church that seeks to minister to many people over time must be ecumenical, confessional, and missional. That is true for local congregations and even more for denominations. The choice is not to be one kind of church or another exclusively, but to represent the fullness of the Christian life appropriately under present conditions.

For individuals, too, the choice should not be seen as a consumer choice, picking an ecumenical, confessional, or missional church as one might choose a make of automobile or a style of dining room furniture. The issue is less a matter of choosing a church that I like than it is creating a church that does not yet exist. If we build well, we will find our faith strengthened, and we will be part of a church that grows and changes to meet the needs of the people among whom it lives.

That relationship between the Christian search for the good life and the wider community beyond the church, however, poses its own set of ethical challenges and opportunities. Those are the issues to which we must now turn.

CHAPTER 6

Society

Christians have worried from the beginning about how to relate the families and churches that shape their search for a good life to the other groups and powers around them. Already in the New Testament we see Jesus' early followers asking how their life as Christians relates to their obligations to the tax collector (Matt 17:24-27) and their social relationships with their non-Christian neighbors (1 Corinthians 8–9).

Of course, for many Christians throughout history, these questions had little practical meaning. Poverty, slavery, or persecution severely limited their choices about their lives and forced them to live their faith as best they could. In the United States before the Civil War, African slaves gathered away from the eyes of their white masters to sing spirituals and listen to the Exodus story. Russian believers found ways to conduct worship, offer the sacraments, and even provide theological instruction and ordination in Soviet prison camps. Chinese Christians worshiped in house churches, secreted from a suspicious culture and a hostile state and cut off from contact with Christians in other parts of the world. These examples, and many others, testify to the resilience of the Christian life under even the most hostile circumstances.

Those who have had more choice in the matter have often thought that they should separate Christian life as much as possible from the temptations and constraints of the surrounding culture. We have noted that the preference for a contemplative life rather than an active life was already present among thoughtful people in the ancient world.[1] This led some Christians even before 300 CE to abandon cities for crude settlements in the desert where they could devote themselves to prayer and reflection. The exaltation of the contemplative life flourished in the monastic movements of the Middle Ages, as thousands of men and women left secular life for cloisters, where their daily routines could be regulated by their religious devotion.

The Protestant Reformation rejected monasticism and put new emphasis on the importance of family life and earning a living, but the

Reformers stressed that these worldly obligations were supports for Christian living, not ends in themselves. Christians pursued trades and built homes to supply the means for a godly life and to protect themselves and their families from the temptations that awaited those who had to make their lives in the markets, the public houses, and the streets. Politics and government, especially, were tasks that Christians could take on only as a service to their neighbors. Government might be able to restrain evil, but Luther and other leaders of the Reformation did not expect it to accomplish very much good.[2]

No doubt there are many people today who think of Christian life as something that they live primarily in the family and the church. With so many conflicting messages at work, on the airwaves, and in the culture, these Christians think it is best to center their lives where they can hear the Word of God clearly. That accounts in part, perhaps, for the growing popularity of church programs that provide opportunities for social life, exercise, recreation, and family activities along with prayer, worship, and Bible study. Best to keep as much of life as possible under one roof where the values are clear. Venturing beyond the home and the community of faith is a risky business, as many Christians see it. The rest of the world may be a good place to witness, but it is a dangerous place to listen, and we cannot expect to accomplish much there.

"Render unto Caesar . . . "

Although this suspicion is deeply rooted in Christian history, we have to ask whether it is adequate for our situation today. Modern democracy makes the people responsible for much of what government does or fails to do. While many Christians in the United States now say they have low expectations for their political leaders, there is some truth in the saying that in a democracy the people get the leaders they deserve. Today, too, most of us readily accept the wider range of opportunities and choices that modern life offers us in our personal lives. We should not ignore the similar expansion of possibilities in public life. Living the Christian life today requires us to rethink the connection between faith and society in ways that most Christian groups have not done since the Reformation. The result may well be the discovery that the world we enter when we leave home and church is not a threat to our faith, but a place where faith must be lived if it is to be complete. Faith may be at risk in the world, but it is also risky to shelter it from the world. Faith that is insulated from the full range of human interactions may be weak and incomplete, and it may easily become confused with the prejudices that just happen to be strongest in those places where I think my faith is safest.

We might rethink this question about the Christian moral life for our time by returning to the beginning, to a story from Jesus' ministry in which he is asked whether it is lawful to pay taxes to the Roman emperor. Jesus confounds his opponents, who wanted to trick him into defying the authorities, by pointing out that the coin with which the tax is paid bears the emperor's head and his inscription. So, Jesus says, in the familiar words of the King James Bible, "Render therefore unto Caesar the things which are Caesar's; and unto God the things that are God's" (Matt 22:21 KJV).

This story appears in all three of the synoptic Gospels (Matt 22:15-22; Mark 12:13-17; Luke 20:20-26), and it has been important from the earliest days of the church, though it has had a number of different uses. In the early church it probably reinforced the message that Christians were not dangerous subversives, but law-abiding citizens who respected authority and paid their taxes. The same idea appears in Romans 13:5-7 and again in 1 Peter 2:13-15, where the point is put very plainly: "For the Lord's sake accept the authority of every human institution, whether of the emperor as supreme, or of governors, as sent by him to punish those who do wrong and to praise those who do right. For it is God's will that by doing right you should silence the ignorance of the foolish."

Since the Reformation this passage has been used primarily to support a sharp distinction between church and state. Both religious and secular leaders have their specific powers given by God, and it is as important to give each the respect it is due as it is to be sure that each does not intrude on the other's sphere of authority. The church must not wield coercive power, and the state must not dictate religious belief. This separation was used sometimes to protect the state from the power of the church and sometimes to protect the church from the power of the state; but it runs consistently through Protestant thought from Luther's time through the men of English Protestant ancestry who framed the First Amendment to the Constitution of the United States, which forbids Congress to make a law "respecting an establishment of religion, or prohibiting the free exercise thereof."

The original point of the story, however, seems not to have been so narrowly drawn. To be sure, it begins with people who have come to Jesus with a question about paying taxes to the Roman authorities, but the question can hardly have been a modern one about church and state. In fact, the question is a trick, intended to draw Jesus into saying something that would get him in trouble. The premise is that Jesus' devotion to God is so complete that he will not compromise with the emperor's demands, so that if his opponents can just find a question that really puts him on the spot, he will walk right into the trap. All they have to do is play on his sincerity and single-minded commitment. "So they sent their disciples to him, along with the Herodians, saying, 'Teacher, we know that you are sincere, and teach the way of God in accordance with truth, and show deference to no one, for you do not regard people with partiality. Tell us, then, what you think. It is lawful to pay taxes to the emperor, or not?' " (Matt 22:16-17).

The dilemma seems inescapable to the Pharisees and the Herodians: Jesus has demanded complete devotion to God. Now he will either have to compromise that commitment and show that he is no different from the rest of the collaborators, or he will have to hold to his position and bring the wrath of the authorities down on himself. It is a neat trick, but Jesus just as neatly evades it. He asks to see the coin with which the tax would be paid. "Then he said to them, 'Whose head is this, and whose title?' They answered, 'The emperor's.' Then he said to them, 'Give therefore to the emperor the things that are the emperor's, and to God the things that are God's' " (Matt 22:20-21).

It was a good answer to a trick question, but the answer has a serious point too. Jesus lives a life of complete devotion to God, but that devotion is no protection from the demands of other authorities who will require a response on their own terms—taxes to be paid, services to be rendered, promises to be kept, rules to be obeyed. Unless we attempt the path of complete withdrawal from society, we will have to answer a whole series of questions about how our faith in God relates to the more immediate powers, authorities, and relationships that are part of everyday life, questions like the one the disciples of the Pharisees and the Herodians put to Jesus: "Is it lawful to . . . ?" Jesus' answer suggests that it is no compromise with the sincerity of our faith to answer "Yes" to such a question, but the answer can never be an unqualified "Yes."

Competing, potentially conflicting, obligations are a normal part of human life; and the problem isn't confined to the more modern conflict between church and state. Any institution that requires our loyalty may make excessive demands. History warns us that the state is prone to do so, but in our experience it is more likely to be an employer who has us wondering how to render to the business what belongs to it while reserving for God what belongs to God. Our families and our friendships require much of us. We give to them out of love and gratitude as well as obligation, and we regard people who withhold things from their friends and families as selfish. But we must not give our families and friends everything. How much can we give to them before we have to be reminded to give God what belongs to God? Even the church can pose the question for us. The church is an important point of connection to God; and it rightly asks for our prayers, presence, gifts, and service. At some point, however, the church's claim can become too exclusive, and it starts demanding loyalty that belongs only to God. When must we also say, "Give to the church what belongs to the church, and give to God what belongs to God"?

Christian faith is not an alternative, undivided loyalty that answers all these questions before they are asked. Christian faith takes the competing obligations seriously, but it turns aside the trick questions that treat faith and other commitments as exclusive choices, as though love for God denies respect to Caesar. The key is to give each relationship the loyalty it deserves, and to hold all of them in proper alignment with one another.

Divine Mandates

Dietrich Bonhoeffer provided a way of thinking about this issue that speaks to the complex form that these conflicts take in our time. Bonhoeffer died at age 39 for his part in the resistance to the Nazi regime in Germany. The last years of his brief, but brilliant, career as a theologian were spent helping the church to survive war and repression. Bonhoeffer understood, however, that the struggle of the German churches raised issues that apply not only in those extreme conditions, but at all times. At the height of the Second World War, he was already looking forward to the postwar world, where he saw that people would need new ways of thinking about their society, first in Germany, but also throughout Europe and in North America too.

Bonhoeffer began with the Lutheran tradition's sharp distinction between religious and secular authority; and he was among the leaders of the Confessing Church, which resisted the Nazi effort to mix Christian faith with German nationalism. Bonhoeffer never relaxed that opposition; but over the course of the struggle, he saw that more was involved than the question of church versus state. Other institutions and loyalties were also affected by the conflict. Families were undermined, schools lost their freedom to teach and pursue truth. Cultural institutions were forced to glorify the achievements of the German state. Businesses were put at the service of its military power.

A whole human life is lived in a variety of settings where goals are set, commitments are made, and obligations are accepted. Because everyone depends on families, churches, schools, cultural institutions, and businesses for the opportunities that make it possible to live a good life, all of us are concerned that these institutions do their work well. We also need them to work harmoniously with each other. We cannot easily live a good life if we are part of a society that undermines its families, sets its schools at odds with its government, or exploits its cultural resources for commercial purposes. A good life, as we have seen, is built around a diversity of goods and goals. We need this complex system of interdependent, yet distinct, institutions in order to set the goals and plans that will give us a good life.

Bonhoeffer called these institutions the "divine mandates."[3] They are places where the Word of God can be heard and give guidance to life. So it is not just that we hear the Word of God proclaimed in church and take it into the marketplace, the school, and the government office. We learn something about the Word of God in and through our participation in these mandates as well as in the Word proclaimed to them.

There is no universal agreement on how these divine mandates should be named. Bonhoeffer and other theologians have provided several different lists, but the basic idea is clear: Human beings, with their irreducibly different goods and goals, need several quite different settings in which to work together on lasting goals. The state, with its laws, courts, legislatures, and administrative agencies, is one such institution. The world of work is another. We need employers, labor unions, professional associations, stock markets, banks, and a myriad of other institutions to maintain the productive process and give people a way to participate in it. Intimate relationships with family and friends form yet another area of life, one that is the most important for many people, and one that requires both support by and protection from government and the world of work. Education serves the needs of both state and business, but it is also different from either of them; and it requires support from other institutions that maintain cultural heritages and encourage artistic creativity. The church and other religious institutions relate closely to family and to education, but they also supply spiritual needs that also affect how we relate to work and to government; and unlike cultural institutions that focus on human creativity, churches, synagogues, mosques, and temples build relationships to God and provide opportunities for worship.

The details may differ, but some such list will serve as a guide to what Bonhoeffer had in mind when he spoke of divine mandates. Government, work, education and culture, family and friendship, and religion are places in our lives where the Word of God can be heard in different ways. We need to find our place in each of these mandates in order to understand God's will for our lives in its fullness, and we need all of the mandates to work together.

The list of mandates is open to interpretation, and so is the problem of exactly how the Word of God is heard in the mandates. Bonhoeffer's work, which he never had an opportunity to revise or complete, has elements of all three of the approaches to moral rules—divine command, covenant, and natural law—that we reviewed in chapter 3. Ethical theorists continue to debate which of these approaches should be primary; but for most Christians seeking to live a good life, the questions are closer to Bonhoeffer's practical concerns. We are less concerned with a theory about the divine mandates than we are to know how we can tell when they are not working and what we can do to restore them.

The mandates serve as reliable guides to the moral life only when they are working well and working in proper relationship to one another. In a dysfunctional family people fail to provide one another with the intimacy and trust they need to develop full human personalities. But a dysfunctional family also teaches people the wrong things about God because the failure of love in these basic human relationships can make it all but impossible to understand God as a loving father or a nurturing mother. Given enough dysfunctional families over a long enough time, the schools will begin to suffer because students will not be prepared for the discipline education requires and will lack the self-confidence to pursue new goals. Eventually this takes its toll in turn on the world of work.

When one of the mandates is too strong or too weak, none of the others can function as it should. That, Bonhoeffer saw, was the problem in Nazi Germany. The state was trying to govern and to educate and to direct the economy. To do all that, it had to control the family, and it had to eliminate competing ideas from the culture. Ultimately, it had to make sure that religious life in the churches did not support any independent loyalties that reached beyond the nation. Family, culture, and faith that could not conform had to be broken or, in the case of the Jews, destroyed. Parents feared to speak honestly to their children, and children were taught at school to mistrust their parents. People were deprived of their livelihood and set to work for the purposes of the state. Fear silenced authors and artists who were not already driven into exile or imprisoned.

The situation in which Bonhoeffer lived was extreme, but its extremity pointed up distortions that can take milder forms in societies that are not at war or undergoing a totalitarian takeover. Work can supplant family and probe into the intimate details of individual lives. Families, schools, and churches can get into competition over the education of children. Cultural creativity can wither for want of economic resources or be suppressed by religious controversy. If we have any hope of leading a good life, even in the relatively favorable circumstances that most of the readers of this book live in, we will have to work with others to ensure that the mandates function as they should. Along with defining the goals and plans that make up each of our own ideas of the good life, we have this moral task that we share with all of our neighbors.

Realism

In thinking about how society and its institutions should work to sustain the possibility of a good life for everyone, we need also to be thoughtful about what we expect. This is especially true for Christians and others who not only have personal plans and goals that they hope to achieve, but also share a missional understanding of how the world needs to be changed to reflect the way of life for which God created us and to which God calls us.[4]

Those who seek to build the kingdom of God have a powerful motivation for the hard work and self-sacrifice that mission requires. They have a long heritage from which to draw images and examples of the changes they seek. But they are also susceptible to the characteristic mistakes made by people who have important dreams. They may confuse their dream with a plan and come up with solutions that are too simple for complex problems, as though poverty and injustice could be eradicated if everyone just shared a little more. They are apt to think they can persuade people to do what is right by words alone and to overlook the need to use power to get people to do what is not in their immediate self-interest. Because they are committed to a goal that they also understand as God's mission, they may find it hard to face their mistakes and limitations; and they are tempted to treat anyone who opposes them as an enemy of God.

The result is that Christians who are concerned to live their faith often aim very high and then fall far short of the goal. Achieving only part of a splendid vision may still be a good thing, but there is a real risk that large goals and strong commitments will end up accomplishing less than more modest efforts might have done. A moral crusade that leaves its followers exhausted and disillusioned, its opponents angry and resistant to future change, and its goals largely unachieved may actually set back the purposes it intended to serve.

It is not too much to say that this has been the problem of Christian social ethics in America in the twentieth century. The century began with Rauschenbusch's Social Gospel hope for a transformation that really would begin a new world and make even the social progress of the nineteenth century look "semi-barbarous" by comparison.[5] Instead, the moral idealists of Europe and North America blundered into the First World War, and their inability to deal with the realities of worldwide depression and resurgent nationalism that followed hastened the arrival of the Second World War. A great moral movement toward racial equal-ity, culminating in Martin Luther King Jr.'s (1929–68) triumphant "I have a dream" speech at the Lincoln Memorial, faded toward the end of the century because of a failure to deal with underlying economic inequalities, persistent residential segregation, and a proliferation of interest groups, each staking its own claim to the territory that had previously been occupied by others.

Reinhold Niebuhr (1892–1971) saw this problem clearly in the aftermath of the First World War, and he called on Christians to give up their appealing moral idealism for a more tough-minded Christian Realism that would pay attention to the real dynamics of social change as well as to the ideal goals of peace and justice.[6] Niebuhr's point, however, was not just that Christians have to be more realistic in their dealings with others. They also have to be more realistic about themselves. They need to understand how their Christian faith is mixed up with their cultural prejudices and with their interest in the place they occupy in their own society. They need to hear the gospel not only as it is preached in their own churches, but also as it is read and heard by other people who do not share their prejudices, who live under very different conditions or in other parts of the world. They need to understand their resistance to change, and if they are able to change themselves and their communities, they must then find ways to make those same changes acceptable to others whose interests and beliefs may be very different from their own.

If we understand our situation in this way, we will see at once that the ancient aspiration to withdraw into a community where the Christian life can be lived in its pure form is not a plausible solution to the complexities of life in society. Christians do not stand at the edge of their society, testing its temperature by a pure biblical standard to decide whether or not it is safe to jump in. We are already in it with both feet when we first ask the question. The very way that we see its problems and failures—and the problems and failures that we do not see or choose to ignore—are the products of both our Christian faith and our social experience. We can develop a critical perspective on that starting point, and we will need to do so if we are to work effectively for change; but we cannot jump out of our skins. The kind of community that we seek to create will always reflect the vision of God's reign that we share with other Christians throughout history and the limitations imposed by our starting point.

The Christian Realist, in short, focuses on what actually is and not just on what ought to be. Niebuhr once defined this kind of realism as "the disposition to take all factors in a social and political situation, which offer resistance to established norms, into account, particularly the factors of self-interest and power."[7] That does not mean that our shared moral ideals, the established norms of which Niebuhr speaks, are irrelevant. He was in fact very clear that without the power of those ideals to motivate us and make our actions less selfish and more loving than they otherwise would be, our political life would quickly become nothing but a battleground of competing interests, with nothing to hold it together except the wary attention we give to those whose actions we do not trust. For Niebuhrian Realists, politics—especially international politics during the long cold war confrontation between the United States and the Soviet Union—often did appear to approximate that grimly realistic model; but Niebuhr believed that the democratic ideals of liberty and equality play a role too.[8]

The practical point is that the moral idealist must not leap at plans that promise to realize all of the ideals all at once. That is unlikely to be successful; and if it were to work, the results might not be desirable, since any specific version of the ideal will have blind spots and limitations and will create its own problems if it is implemented without qualifications. An effective Christian Realist, therefore, will chart out short, incremental steps toward the larger goal, concentrating at each step on the obstacles of self-interest and power that have to be overcome at this point. And because Christian Realists understand that their vision has limitations, they will be more likely to build coalitions around specific short-term goals and plans than to demand complete allegiance to the whole vision from the outset.

Justice and Power

Christian Realists in the mold of Reinhold Niebuhr are acute analysts of what is actually happening in society. Niebuhr became one of the most important public figures of his generation, not because many people agreed with his theology, but because he understood so well the powers and interests at work in the controversies of his day. He pointed the way to effective political solutions and strategic alliances in a world where both national and international politics were dominated by powerful groups with competing interests.

In recent years, however, Christian ethics has given more attention to those who are unlikely to figure in a realistic calculation of power and interest. The elderly poor, often confined to home and confused by the changes going on around them, may have much at risk in those changes; but they are unlikely on their own to acquire much power to affect the outcomes. Working poor people, often single parents with great needs and limited resources, may be too exhausted by the tasks of daily living to think very much about what they might accomplish in coalitions with others who share their problems. Homeless people and undocumented workers who have come from other countries often lack even the most minimal resources to claim the attention of more powerful people who might be in a position to do something for them. People who are physically or mentally challenged may not be able to organize their lives or join forces with others in ways that will make their needs felt.

Living as we do in a society that includes many people in these situations, it is not enough simply to understand the configurations of interest and power that now exist. Christian ethics has a special concern for those who need an advocate to ensure that their interests are known and included in the calculations by which society allocates its resources.

That concern has a long history. In medieval Europe monasteries cared for the poor and the sick when there were no other institutions for them. Christian missions have often begun by caring for these basic human needs, even before they turn to teaching and preaching; and partly as a result, Christian faith has often spread most rapidly among those who occupied the lowest places in the societies where the missionaries found them. Churches in inner cities and rural communities maintain food pantries and provide emergency household supplies for the growing number of those who have dropped out of the economic system or slipped through the social safety net that is supposed to provide these necessities.

These efforts to alleviate individual needs will continue to be important, but we have come to understand more clearly that they are not all that is required. Problems of disease and poverty that have received the church's charitable attention through the centuries are now seen not only as needs to be met with healing and compassion, but also as evils that can be prevented. Although we are, perhaps, not as optimistic as Walter Rauschenbusch and the early preachers of the Social Gospel about our ability to master these social problems completely, we can no longer accept the suffering they cause as inevitable. Ministry to human need now includes social and political strategies to prevent suffering as well as charitable responses to relieve it where it already exists.

More generally, both the church and the wider society have come to accept that in some basic respects all persons are equal. Each deserves to be treated with respect for his or her personal integrity and with care for possibilities that allow him or her to lead a good life. The idea began with the spread of democracy in the eighteenth century and grew to include not only political freedoms, but also claims on basic goods that everyone needs in order to live whatever life seems good to them.[9] The result has been a concept of universal human rights to which every person is entitled and a growing acceptance of the idea that the international community can hold governments and political leaders accountable when those rights are denied.[10]

In the United States the social concerns of the churches throughout the twentieth century have largely been with securing justice for those whose needs society fails to recognize and those whose access to basic goods has been denied. In the 1920s John A. Ryan applied traditional Roman Catholic social teaching to modern industrial society and came up with the concept of a "living wage" to which all working families are entitled. America's Roman Catholic bishops returned to those themes in 1986 with a pastoral letter on economic justice.[11] In the 1930s the NAACP initiated a series of lawsuits that resulted in three decades of court orders and legislative action to secure racial justice for African American citizens. Churches and synagogues were centrally involved in this effort, both in support of legal decisions and legislative changes and in the mass movements and demonstrations that made these changes real on the local level. Dr. Martin Luther King, Jr., became a key voice for this form of justice and equal opportunity, both in the church and in the wider society. Speaking for the people marching for desegregation in 1962, he said, "We feel that we are the conscience of America—we are its troubled soul—we will continue to insist that right be done because both God's will and the heritage of our nation speak through our echoing demands."[12]

By the end of King's life, however, a new note could be heard in the demands for justice. More and more, those who had been excluded from participation in important parts of society were insisting not only on admission to the opportunities generally available to others, but also on the power to define their own identity and to participate in setting the terms on which social institutions would operate. As an earlier call to meet human need through charity developed into a demand for justice, that demand grew to include empowerment as well as equal opportunity.

This new development required theologians to rethink social issues in important ways. Niebuhr's Christian Realism had warned the powerful that their idea of justice was distorted by their place in society. The new group of theologians concerned about empowerment understood from the outset that their experiences of exclusion and oppression had shaped their ideas about justice; but for them, it was precisely this new perspective that needed to be heard, a "voice from below" that promised a more complete assessment of what justice requires than the equal access to existing opportunities that the authorities in business and government were offering. One of King's later essays, published after his death, strikes the theme: "White America must recognize that justice for black people cannot be achieved without radical changes in the structure of our society. The comfortable, the entrenched, the privileged cannot continue to tremble at the prospect of a change in the status quo."[13]

It fell to others to make a case for those radical changes during the last three decades of the twentieth century. For theologians, the rethinking has included both the requirements of justice and the fundamental relationship between faith and power in the Christian tradition. If the gospel is addressed, not to those who already have power, but to those who have been deprived of it, then the good news may include the unexpected fact that God is with them in their struggle for empowerment. "There can be no comprehension of the gospel apart from God's solidarity with the liberation struggles of the poor," wrote African American theologian James H. Cone, "because the freedom of the victims on earth is the eschatological sign of God's intention to redeem the whole creation."[14] If, on the other hand, the authority of the gospel is not to be confused with the forms of authority and power that prevail in contemporary society, then it may be necessary to rethink the whole relationship between biblical faith and the language of gender, as Beverly Harrison has urged us to do.[15]

Relating justice and empowerment has brought new voices of women and minorities to the attention of both church and society; and nearly every congregation has experienced leadership in the pulpit, the classroom, and the committee meeting that would not have been heard there a generation or two before. We have also become aware of voices from the global church, and not just the European theologians who have received the attention of American pastors and scholars in the past. Latin American liberation theology, especially the work of Gustavo Gutiérrez, has inspired many in North America and Europe to attempt reading the Bible in their own social context, which has proved so important in freeing communities of the poor in Latin America to overcome their powerlessness.[16]

The relationships between charity, justice, and empowerment remain controversial in the church and in society at large. When confidence in the power of government and large organizations to solve our problems wanes, people speak of returning to a time when human needs were met on a small scale, in families, churches, and local communities. When large disparities in wealth, income, and access to power between men and women or between whites and minority group members persist after decades of affirmative action and equal opportunity procedures, suggestions are made for a still more radical redistribution of wealth and opportunity. It is unlikely that our society or our churches will reach consensus on these issues anytime soon, and the questions they raise will continue to provide the context in which many more specific policy choices have to be made.

Politics

The end of the twentieth century finds us with many of the same social problems that faced us at its beginning. Violent conflict between

113

individuals and war between nations, which the preachers of the Social Gospel hoped would be ended by general prosperity, remain with us despite technological advances that could hardly be imagined a hundred years ago. The search for opportunity and dignity for all people has made progress, as colonialism has ended and democracy has spread, and more workers enjoy more of the results of their labor. But this progress is not complete, and it has raised troubling new questions about the relationships between human dignity and political power and about the tension between minority empowerment and inclusive community.

Alongside these very old questions there are the new problems created by the technology and economic growth that were once expected to provide all the solutions. We may have learned to manage the cycles of expansion and contraction in the domestic economy, but these techniques will now have to become global if they are to provide any real economic security for people whose jobs and savings depend on markets in Indonesia and interest rates in Europe. The effects of production, transportation, and the concentration of people in large urban centers must now be calculated in terms of their impact on ecosystems that extend across national boundaries. Technological solutions to today's problems must be assessed for their sustainability for future generations. Computers, medical science, and mass communications put new powers in our hands before we can fully understand their effects on our lives or their long-term consequences for the future of humanity.

Our efforts to live a good life inevitably take these changes and problems into account. We may be grateful that we do not face the limited medical options that our great-grandparents had, even though we often have to cope with higher levels of stress and change in our daily lives than they ever faced; and we have to deal with knowledge about diet, health, and nutrition that they never had. We worry about personal security in places where previous generations never locked their doors, but we also know that we have had a great many more choices about how to live our lives and how to make a living than those people had. And despite some worries about the trajectory for economic expansion, most of us expect that our children will have an even wider range of options than we do. We accept new duties as we learn more about how our actions affect the environment. (How old were you when you learned to sort the trash for recycling?) We reject old prejudices as social changes propel us into new sorts of relationships. (How many of us could get through the work week if we had held on to the racial attitudes of our parents? What ideas of ours will our children need to move beyond to work in the world they will enter?) Our understanding of what a good life is changes with the world around us, and so our ethics changes too.

But the ethical issues that lie behind these changes are not questions that we can resolve individually. They impinge on the possibility of a good life so directly that we have to make individual responses to them, but the larger impact they have on everyone's possibilities can only be addressed by what we do together. Even thinking together about a Christian response to the global economy or to the ecological crisis isn't likely to provide more than a step toward the solutions in a world that includes such a diversity of religious and moral perspectives. The decisions we make about our personal ethics and the conclusions we reach when we think about moral questions together as Christians must become part of a larger discussion if they are going to make the difference we would want to make for the future.

Large volumes have been written on each of these problems, and this brief introduction to ethics cannot even survey the issues surrounding ecological ethics, welfare reform, nuclear weapons, and medical care at the end of life. We have, however, learned some things in this book about how to begin thinking about such questions as Christians and about how to relate that thinking to the issues and choices that are debated in the wider society in which we live.

On many issues the biblical witness to which Christian discussion always returns provides us with a starting point—not so much a rule or a policy, but an attitude that gets our thinking started in the right direction and helps us to ask the right questions. When the Roman Catholic bishops in the United States wanted to address issues of economic justice, they began with the observation that biblical thinking about justice draws attention first to the way that a society deals with the powerless: "Central to the biblical presentation of justice is that the justice of a community is measured by its treatment of the powerless in society, most often described as the widow, the orphan, the poor, and the stranger (non-Israelite) in the land."[17]

Further investigation of how an agrarian society in the ancient Near East treated its widows and orphans is unlikely to provide specific recommendations for welfare policy in postindustrial North America. But attentiveness to the biblical idea of justice may keep us from falling into the highly individualistic, modern idea that justice simply means protecting everyone's enjoyment of the property they have been able to acquire, or the even harsher notion, espoused by Social Darwinists at the end of the nineteenth century, that nature uses poverty to weed out those who are unable to make a worthwhile contribution to the future of the race. The biblical starting point is not without ambiguities. There are plenty of passages we could choose that would suggest a vindictive attitude toward our enemies or harsh retribution for those who fall short of our moral expectations. But on the whole, those who approach the Bible openly and live with it intimately over time learn a humility that limits their self-righteousness and a compassion that cares first for those who have the least power to defend themselves. Christians who have learned that from the Bible have a direction for further thinking about these problems, and they bring that commitment to the choices about policy that they share with all the rest of their neighbors.

In other cases the Christian tradition provides a highly developed history of moral thinking about specific social questions. Much has been written, for example, about the extent and limits of rights to one's personal property in the face of extreme human need, about the obligations that people owe to one another in the context of family life, and about the relationships between church and state. Those who are interested in these issues can trace their development in a literature that goes back through centuries of Christian moral thought. Nowhere is this more widely recognized than in the long tradition, extending at least back to Augustine, about the moral use of force in war. Successive generations of writers have refined the criteria that can justify the decision to make war in the first place as well as the criteria that limit the use of force once the war is underway. Exactly how these guidelines are to be applied must be rethought in each new situation, but when decisions have had to be made about the morality of nuclear deterrence or about the justification of military intervention in the Persian Gulf, analysts both Christian and non-Christian have turned to the framework provided by the just war tradition to understand the choices they had to make in a contemporary setting.[18]

Often, however, the moral problems we face are quite new, or at least they cannot easily be cast in the framework provided by previous moral thought. These are often the most perplexing and divisive issues because we feel not only that we do not know how to defend our opinions, but also that we do not really know how to begin a discussion with those who disagree with us. Yet even here we are not without some guidance. Those Christian ethicists who have struggled with serious social problems through the course of this century have provided at least some points that need to be considered as we try to resolve the difficult problems that are peculiar to our own time. Bonhoeffer, Niebuhr, King, Cone, Harrison, and Gutiérrez do not provide a single set of answers; but if we are not at least asking the questions that they asked, the answers we arrive at are apt to be incomplete and misleading.

Bonhoeffer reminds us that Christian ethics can never be conducted in isolation from the context of institutions in which people are seeking to live good lives. Understanding what we must do to make good lives possible begins with the knowledge and experience that people have in government, family life, work, church, and education. We cannot make

116

pronouncements about their lives and work from a distance, as though the seriousness of our moral purposes could substitute for a detailed appreciation of the actual situation and the specialized knowledge that is required to deal with it. That is why Bonhoeffer asks us to listen for the Word of God within the mandates and not simply to address the Word to them. We should be suspicious of any moral system that tells us to abandon the vocations we have accepted, the covenants with other people that we have made, or the obligations of citizenship. There are times when these things must be set aside, but leaping outside of the ordinary framework in which human life is lived is rarely, if ever, the first step in social ethics. Social ethics asks first how institutions really work and what would be required to make them work better.

For institutions to work, of course, they have to work together. That was what Bonhoeffer saw most clearly in the fearful success of a totalitarian state that destroyed the other mandates alongside it. Once we have understood the internal requirements of government, family, work, and education, we need to pay attention to those places at the margins where each tends to encroach upon the others. A good deal of Christian social ethics can be conducted within this framework suggested by Bonhoeffer's analysis. What does a physician's work require from the society? What level of regulation can it tolerate from the business practices required to sustain a hospital or an insurance system? Can government secure justice for patients without undermining these internal requirements of medical practice? Or, to turn to another mandate, what role does the family play in shaping the moral life of children so that they can live good lives as adults? How far can the family's control go before it undermines the exploration of the world that is essential to education? When does education raise so many questions that it undermines the moral role of the family? The answers are not obvious, and arriving at them will require much patient listening that extends across the usual boundaries of race, social class, and religious identity. But Christians who have learned something from the church's wrestling with social issues through the twentieth century will at least understand the importance of paying attention to the questions.

They may also have learned from Reinhold Niebuhr to be realistic about their interest in the answers. Our willingness to change depends in part on considered judgments about what institutions require to function well, but it also depends on how well we are served by the way things work now. Christian Realism leads us to examine the interests that are at work in a social situation as well as the ideals we bring to it.

Two results follow from this kind of realism. First, as a practical matter, we will not expect people to give up power or accept others into their communities just because we have demonstrated that that is what they ought to do. Realistic thinking about how to make institutions work better involves asking what kind of power will be needed for people to accept the changes. It involves asking not only who shares our moral ideals in their pure form, but also who might be interested in a coalition that would accomplish part of what we both seek in the present, even if we disagree about the ultimate goals. Second, every moral solution is a combination of ideals and interests. It reflects both the situation we are trying to understand and the interests of the people who are trying to understand it. So it will not surprise a Christian Realist to learn that few, if any, answers to the questions of social ethics are final. They do not have the precision of answers to problems in physics or accounting, and even the best of them require correction over time. Demands for justice usually begin with people who want equality; but after a while the constraints required to secure equality begin to chafe, and insistent voices will then demand more freedom. This does not mean that the first demands for justice were wrong. It does not mean that any claim is as good as any other nor does it render all moral claims meaningless. It does require us to be aware of historical circumstances when we make moral judgments and to pay close attention to all the interests that are at work in the situation, including our own.

We should not accept the sentimental notion that moral discussions are the work of people who have abandoned their own interests. But we should be aware that there will be those who lack the power and the opportunity to make their interests felt in the same way that we do. Indeed, they may lack the education or the experience to make their interests known in terms that fit into a political campaign or a public policy debate, so we will not even know they are there unless we learn to listen to their stories and their songs, to hear them tell about their lives in their own terms. What we learn from liberation and feminist theologians is that an understanding of institutions and a realistic assessment of interests may still overlook some people who have an important stake in how society answers its questions.

Justice and empowerment are not issues that are restricted to the poor and those who work with them. They ought to affect the way all of us think about society. Most people who read and write books on Christian ethics have jobs that give them a quite specific place in one of Bonhoeffer's mandates. That knowledge and experience may be the most important thing they have to contribute to Christian thinking about society. But whatever our vocation may be in that sense, all Christians have this calling too: We are to remember those who would otherwise be forgotten and raise our voices for those who would otherwise be silenced.[19] Without that, both our understanding of justice and our attempt to live a good life will be incomplete.

When Christians have thought through a social issue, guided by these perspectives from contemporary Christian ethics, their goals for society may be significantly changed from the ideas with which they began and significantly different from the goals and values held by others who have lower expectations or more narrow interests. The vision and commitment that emerges from Christian reflection is very important. It needs to be celebrated in the churches and lifted up in public, so that there will be no mistake about the standard of justice to which Christians hold themselves and their society accountable.

But Christian vision should not be taken in any simple way as a political platform or as a policy recommendation. Turning Christian social ethics into a program is unrealistic in two ways. First, it is unlikely to succeed. The diversity of groups and interests in our society is so great and the sources of power and influence brought to bear on any important issue are so many that no one's vision gets turned into action without significant changes and compromises. Christians who begin with the expectation that their ideal for the Christian life will become social reality are inevitably disappointed. They may then become angry and disillusioned, abandoning their social concerns altogether, or using increasingly aggressive tactics to coerce where they were unable to persuade. Politics, they may conclude, is inevitably corrupt, and society is too far gone from Christian principles to be led back to them by ordinary means. The problem, however, lies not in politics or in society, but in their own unrealistic expectations. Political gains, even for the most noble purposes, are made a step at a time; and the end result rarely corresponds to the blueprint, no matter how carefully or prayerfully the plans have been drawn.

Confusing Christian ethics with a political program is unrealistic in another sense too. It ignores the basic insight of Christian Realism that even our most thoughtful accounts of biblical justice are still limited by our self-interested starting points. That means that we are subject to correction, not just by our allies and those who stand closest to us, but also by our opponents. If we really commit ourselves to a Christian understanding of justice in society, we will experience defeats and losses as well as occasional triumphs. Some of those defeats will be real setbacks in which relief for those who suffer is delayed, resources are lost, and opponents of change get a stronger hold on the levers of power. Everyone who has worked for an ideal over a long period of time, however, also knows that some defeats give insight into the weak points in our vision and show us the places where our goals need revision so that they can serve a more inclusive community. Reinhold Niebuhr put it this way in an early article where he first defined what it is to be a Christian Realist: "The church would do more for the cause of reconciliation if,

119

instead of producing moral idealists who think that they can establish justice, it would create religious and Christian realists who know that justice will require that some men shall contend against them."[20] In those contests, our losses are as important as our victories. For a Christian who seeks to make faith real in a social context, the good life will include both.

Conclusion: Faith and Ethics

We have made a fairly comprehensive survey of the Christian moral life. We began by noting that human beings generally want to live good lives, and they devote a substantial amount of reflective time to thinking about how to do that. They set goals for themselves, so that their energies and talents will not be wasted. They want to accomplish things that are part of the good life they are seeking, and they make plans and choices that they expect to get them to their goals.

These goals are as varied as the people who set them. There is no single ideal for a good life that fits all people. There does not even seem to be a single ideal of the Christian life that fits everyone who is seeking a good life in the context of Christian beliefs and commitments.

But people do learn some things from experience that shape and limit the goals they pursue. They learn early that what seems good at the moment does not always make for a good life over the long run. Goals have to be set with a whole life in mind, even if that means giving up some of the things we want and making substantial sacrifices along the way to reach the goals that are really important. People also learn that the goals they seek are bound up with the lives of other people. At first, they may think this means only that they have to adjust what they want so they will have the cooperation of other people in their efforts to get it, but the real links between human lives and goals lie deeper than that. Our happiness, we find, depends on the good lives of some other people, so that we cannot live a good life if their lives are not good. We discover that there is greater satisfaction in achieving goals that develop talents in us that other people recognize. We learn that the good things we create are more valuable to us when they are also valued by others. Thus, as we put together a good life for ourselves, we find that this good life ties us to all sorts of other people in many different ways. We find ourselves living in covenant with others, pursuing shared commitments that become more important to us than purely personal goals. At some point we may even find that there are some goals that are so important that we would be willing to sacrifice our lives to make it possible for others to have the good we are seeking.

The ways we share our lives and goals with other people are very important; but much of what we do to live a good life has to be negotiated among people with whom we do not have close personal relationships and, indeed, among those with whom we have varying degrees of disagreement and conflict. The search for a good life under these conditions requires us not only to think about our goals, but also to arrive at some rules that will govern how we pursue those goals. Rules set limits. They tell us what we may not do in order to achieve a goal, so that we do not simply use other people as a way to get what we want. They tell us what we have to respect about other people and their goals, whether or not we think that those people have good lives and whether or not we judge their goals to be worthy.

Rules are so central to ethics that many people think the subject consists of little else. The history of Christian ethics offers several different ways of conceiving these rules. Rules may be understood as God's commandments, or they may be regarded as laws that are built into the way that nature works, or they may be interpreted as part of a covenant we make with God and with other people. Each understanding provides a measure of objectivity for moral rules. We cannot change them to suit ourselves, and we cannot set them aside with the excuse that the goals we are pursuing are so important that the rules do not matter. Because rules have this objectivity, we tend to come back to them at points of conflict and uncertainty in the moral life. Rules tell other people what they can expect from us; and when we are in doubt, they can tell us what we ought to expect of ourselves.

Nevertheless, a moral life built on rules alone would hardly qualify as a good life. We need the limits that rules set only because we also have goals, purposes that we follow across a lifetime with real commitment. It is the way we strike the balance between rules and goals that shapes our moral life and makes us the kind of people we are.

Virtues are the third main element in the moral life, along with rules and goals. Virtues provide the vocabulary in which we describe ourselves and other people morally. Virtues vary a great deal over time, of course. We would hardly recognize some of the virtuous types that Aristotle describes as good people. They would seem to us pompous, self-important, and rude. Indeed, we have a hard enough time appreciating some of the virtues that were admired a generation or two back in our own culture. Yet there are some virtues that seem to persist. They take different forms in different people, but we recognize that they are important because they are the habits of choice and action on which the rest of the moral life depends. Classical and Christian traditions together have identified four of these cardinal virtues: temperance, courage, prudence, and justice. Christian writers have also noted that there are some virtues that are particularly important to the Christian life that come to us as God's gifts rather than as habits acquired by practice. Borrowing from the three abiding realities named in 1 Corinthians 13, Christian ethics has named these theological virtues as faith, hope, and love.

Reflection on virtue reminds us that living a good life is not just making a series of good decisions about following the rules and choosing our goals. Living a good life involves becoming a certain kind of person. We could imagine someone who lived a life always on the edge of intemperance, usually fearful in the face of challenge, and often leaning toward pursuit of inappropriate or unjust goals, but who nevertheless managed more often than not to do the right thing. Would we say that this unlikely character was leading a good life? Probably not. Living a good life, it seems, involves becoming a person with qualities that allow others to depend on you to make the right choices. Perhaps even more important, it involves qualities that allow you to depend on yourself in that way too.

Virtue, whether acquired by practice or received as a gift, has to be lived out over a lifetime. So thinking about virtue inevitably leads us on to further reflection about the families and communities that support good lives and give us an opportunity to see virtue in action. We need an intimate community of love and acceptance where we know we will find support, even when life is hard and our attempts to live it well fall short. We need to be part of a community that gives us a clear identity and shows us who we are and what makes us different from others. But we also need to be part of a community that will challenge us to extend our vision to include new people and to live our virtues in new ways. For Christians, both identity and challenge are often to be found in the church, and we have considered three kinds of churches that support the Christian moral life in different ways: the ecumenical church, the confessional church, and the missional church. Or perhaps we should say that these three are different aspects of life in the church, since each meets a need that Christians trying to live a good life in today's world sometimes have and every real church will have to minister to all three of those needs at one time or another.

Christians, however, are not shaped only by their church community. They live in a society that includes many different, interrelated institutions; and their understandings of the good life inevitably include what they have learned through their participation in this wider society.

Theology in the twentieth century has usually affirmed this participation as a way to learn what God requires of us and has resisted the tendency in parts of Christian history to reject society and seek a way to live apart from its demands. But twentieth-century theology has also been realistic enough to warn that participation in society tempts us to confuse the prejudices of our culture with the requirements of our faith. We need a keen eye for our own interests and the interests of others if we are going to make judgments about how a society should support the good life for its people. Christians, especially, must be alert to the needs of those who lack the power to press their own interests and whose voices may be silenced by the power of others. Social transformation will not be accomplished as easily or as completely as some Christians believed it could be at the beginning of the twentieth century, but concern for the issues that shape society is an important part of the Christian moral life nonetheless.

That is the Christian moral life as we have seen it in these pages. Of course, the problem is that our experience of it never flows in the neat, sequential order suggested by this outline. Logically, we may begin with goals in order to make rules and follow rules in order to acquire virtues. But our reflection on the moral life always begins somewhere in the middle, when a new challenge disrupts our personal goals or calls our familiar virtues into question. Indeed, our reflection on the moral life very often begins precisely when we realize that we have failed at it in some important way—when we see that we have been pursuing the wrong goals, when we have failed to live up to a covenant commitment, when we have not had the courage to do what we know we should do.

We do not begin reflecting on the moral life by opening the textbook to page 1 and proceeding in order through the lessons. It is in the nature of ethics that we are always already living the subject when we start to think about it.

It is important to understand that our faith intersects our ethics there, in the midst of life. Too often we think about faith and ethics in a way that locates faith at the beginning or at the end of the system. It is supposed that those who have faith in God receive a clear set of commandments at the outset, so that the moral life becomes a simple matter of doing what we have been told. Or it is supposed, all too simply, that faith in God means belief in a judge who will add up our moral accomplishments at the end, then give us the reward or punishment that we deserve.

Ideas like that make it hard for non-Christians to take the Christian moral life seriously. It seems to them as if we are not trying to live good lives at all, but merely trying to follow a set of rules in hopes of winning some ultimate reward. Perhaps worse, ideas like that make it hard for Christians to understand why their lives include moments of confusion and failure, and hard for them to see that the Christian life also includes freedom, choice, and love.

Christian faith, however, offers a relationship between God and the moral life quite different from the one that so many people imagine. God meets us not only as lawgiver and as judge, but also and primarily as the gracious One who accepts us despite our failure to live up to what the moral life requires of us, and who restores our hope for the future despite our inability to take back what we have already done or make up for what we have failed to do in the past. We encounter this gracious God not at the beginning of our systematic thinking about ethics, but precisely in the pain and confusion of actual moral life. If we accept the grace God offers, we are freed from the weight of our past and our hope is restored. If we refuse it, our moral life is apt to become a self-deceptive exercise in justifying our mistakes and blaming our failures on others. Or we may slide into the despair of moral failure, unable to undo the wrong we have done and without hope for the future. Only a gracious God keeps our actual moral life from becoming a constant measurement of ourselves against a standard we can never meet, anticipating a dreadful judgment we can never escape.

That does not mean that there is no law or judgment in Christian ethics. People have misunderstood God's grace in that way ever since some told Paul that their response to the gospel would be to continue in sin so that grace may abound (Rom 6:1). It does mean, however, that the Christian moral life is not one long preparation for a judgment that lies ahead of us. Judgment has already happened. We know that as soon as we begin to reflect honestly on the life we have already lived. Because that judgment is covered by grace, we are free to reorient our moral lives toward the future rather than continually reviewing the failures of the past. We are free to understand the lives and needs of others, to build relationships and share commitments with them rather than being tied to constant reexamination of ourselves.

When we encounter a gracious God in the midst of actual moral life, that life becomes our own, probably for the very first time. We need no longer live it according to someone else's pattern, but we can find the goals and virtues that allow us to live a good life in our own situation, with the abilities and limitations that we actually have. We are free to live by the rules and commitments that make a good life possible, instead of trying to justify ourselves to someone else, by someone else's rules. So the moral life, instead of being a way to defend ourselves, becomes a way to love our neighbors and a way to love God as well.

Notes

1. Choices

1. Aristotle, *Nicomachean Ethics,* trans. Martin Ostwald (Library of Liberal Arts; Indianapolis: Bobbs-Merrill, 1962), 3.
2. The Greek *makarioi,* which is traditionally translated in English as "blessed," might equally well be translated as "happy."
3. Augustine, *City of God,* ed. David Knowles (Harmondsworth, England: Penguin Books, 1972), 593.

2. Goals

1. From *telos,* the Greek word for "goal."
2. Jeremy Bentham, *An Introduction to the Principles of Morals and Legislation,* ed. Lawrence Lafleur (New York: Hafner, 1948), 2.
3. Charles M. Sheldon, *In His Steps: "What Would Jesus Do?"* (New York: Hurst, 1905).
4. Joseph Fletcher, *Situation Ethics: The New Morality* (Louisville: Westminster John Knox Press, 1997), 77-81. First published, 1966.
5. Aristotle, *Nicomachean Ethics,* trans. Martin Ostwald (Library of Liberal Arts; Indianapolis: Bobbs-Merrill, 1962), 286-95.
6. Ibid., 23-26.
7. Epictetus, *Handbook,* trans. Nicholas White (Indianapolis: Hackett Publishing Company, 1983), 15.
8. Stephen R. Covey, A. Roger Merrill, and Rebecca R. Merrill, *First Things First* (New York: Simon and Schuster, 1994), 19-31.
9. Walter Rauschenbusch, *Christianity and the Social Crisis* (Louisville: Westminster John Knox Press, 1991), 421. First published, 1910.

10. Karl Barth, *The Epistle to the Romans,* trans. Edwyn Hoskyns (London: Oxford University Press, 1933), 517.

3. Rules

1. Note that the term *deontology* pertains to the study (-ology) of what is required (*deon*). It has nothing to do with the negation (de-) of the study of being (ontology).
2. Aristotle, *Nicomachean Ethics,* trans. Martin Ostwald (Library of Liberal Arts; Indianapolis: Bobbs-Merrill, 1962), 131.
3. Thomas Aquinas, *Summa theologiae,* I-II, QQ. 90-114.
4. John Locke (1632–1704) developed this theory of the social contract in a form that was particularly influential on Jefferson, Madison, Hamilton, and other founders of the American republic. Locke himself took a hand in the formulation of the Fundamental Constitutions of Carolina, the first written constitution in North America.

4. Virtues

1. Stanley Hauerwas and David Burrell, "From System to Story: An Alternative Pattern for Rationalization in Ethics," in Stanley Hauerwas, *Truthfulness and Tragedy: Further Investigations in Christian Ethics* (Notre Dame, Ind.: University of Notre Dame Press, 1977), 15-59.
2. Aristotle, *Nicomachean Ethics,* trans. Martin Ostwald (Library of Liberal Arts; Indianapolis: Bobbs-Merrill, 1962), 34.
3. Thomas Aquinas, *Summa theologiae,* I-II, Q. 55, A. 1.
4. Aristotle, *Nicomachean Ethics,* 41-44.
5. Ibid., 97-98.
6. See chapter 3, pp. 45-50.
7. We should note that the identification of these four virtues also had to do with a theory that dates back to ancient Greece, which holds that the human soul has three parts: a vegetative part that maintains biological life, an animal part that acts to protect the person from external threats and fulfill desires, and a rational part that makes choices on the basis of knowledge and understanding. These parts of the soul were identified, respectively, with the virtues of temperance, courage, and prudence, while justice was the virtue by which the rational part of the soul ruled over the rest and kept their requirements in harmony.
8. Exactly how to balance the distribution between meeting basic needs and rewarding individual effort is, of course, a question of justice that societies and institutions have to answer every time they set wages,

impose taxes, provide security in times of unemployment and old age, and offer assistance to the poor.

9. Some theologians would insist that even our ability to recognize these virtues is a gift of grace. To those without this gift, the faith, hope, and love of Christians appears to be a foolish failure of necessary concern for one's own good.

10. See page 65 above.

11. Augustine, *City of God*, ed. David Knowles (Harmondsworth, England: Penguin Books, 1972), 891.

12. Dietrich Bonhoeffer, *Ethics*, trans. Neville Horton Smith (New York: Macmillan, 1965), 61-63.

13. John Wesley, "The Reward of Righteousness," in *Sermons III* (The Works of John Wesley, vol. 3; Nashville: Abingdon Press, 1986) 403-4. On the long history of this idea in Christian theology generally, see Theodore Runyon, *The New Creation: John Wesley's Theology Today* (Nashville: Abingdon Press, 1998), 53-58.

5. Church

1. Early in the twentieth century, Ernst Troeltsch traced the history of these contrasting patterns of a wide Christian community with inclusive criteria for membership and a more narrow Christian community with higher requirements for admission. He called these respectively the "church-type" and the "sect-type" of Christian community. His point was that the two types recur in many different forms through Christian history, and indeed groups tend to transform themselves over time from one type into another. Troeltsch also identifies a third type, more distinctly modern, which he calls the "mystic" type. We are certainly familiar in today's world with persons who are sometimes deeply religious, but whose beliefs are highly personal and who do not easily affiliate themselves with an organized religious group. See Ernst Troeltsch, *The Social Teaching of the Christian Churches*, 2 vols. (Louisville: Westminster John Knox, 1992). First published in German in 1912.

2. Augustine, *City of God*, ed. David Knowles (Harmondsworth, England: Penguin Books, 1972), 45-46.

3. The ways of thinking about the Christian community outlined here owe something to Troeltsch's categories. Ecumenical thinking corresponds roughly to Troeltsch's church-type, while the confessional and missional groups have some characteristics of Troeltsch's sect-type. Because my interest in this chapter is how to understand the organized Christian community, I will not be considering Troeltsch's third, mystic type, at any length.

4. The term comes from the Greek *oikumene,* which means "the inhabited world."

5. The Latin *catholicus* likewise derives from a Greek word which means "general" or "universal."

6. See the section "Our Doctrinal Standards and General Rules," in *The Book of Discipline of The United Methodist Church, 1996* (Nashville: The United Methodist Publishing House, 1996), 57-72. See also *The Book of Concord: Confessions of the Evangelical Lutheran Church,* trans. Theodore Tappert (Philadelphia: Muehlenberg Press, 1959) and *The Constitution of the Presbyterian Church, U.S.A.: Book of Confessions* (Louisville: Office of the General Assembly, 1996).

7. "Theological Declaration Concerning the Present Situation of the German Evangelical Church," in Arthur C. Cochrane, *The Church's Confession Under Hitler* (Philadelphia: Westminster Press, 1962), 239.

8. Dietrich Bonhoeffer, *Life Together/Prayerbook of the Bible,* trans. Daniel Bloesch and James Burtness (Dietrich Bonhoeffer Works, vol. 5; Minneapolis: Fortress Press, 1996).

9. William J. Abraham, "Confessing Christ: A Quest for Renewal in Contemporary Christianity," 51 *Interpretation* (1997), 120.

10. Walter Rauschenbusch, *Christianity and the Social Crisis* (Louisville: Westminster John Knox Press, 1991), 421.

6. Society

1. See chapter 2, page 27.

2. Martin Luther, "Secular Authority: To What Extent It Should Be Obeyed," in John Dillenberger, ed., *Martin Luther: Selections from His Writings* (Garden City, N.Y.: Doubleday, 1961), 368-73.

3. Dietrich Bonhoeffer, *Ethics,* trans. Neville Horton Smith (New York: Macmillan, 1965), 207.

4. See chapter 5, pages 94-99.

5. See chapter 5, page 97.

6. Reinhold Niebuhr, *Moral Man and Immoral Society* (New York: Charles Scribner's Sons, 1933), 231-56.

7. Niebuhr, *The Essential Reinhold Niebuhr: Selected Essays and Addresses,* ed. Robert McAfee Brown (New Haven: Yale University Press, 1986), 123.

8. Niebuhr, "Liberty and Equality" in Ronald Stone, ed., *Faith and Politics* (New York: George Braziller, 1968), 185-97.

9. See chapter 2, page 25.

10. For a good review of these historical developments, see Ian Brownlie, ed. *Basic Documents on Human Rights* (Oxford: Clarendon Press, 1971).

11. John A. Ryan, *A Living Wage* (New York: Macmillan, 1906); National Conference of Catholic Bishops, *Economic Justice for All: Pastoral Letter on Catholic Social Teaching and the U.S. Economy* (Washington, D.C.: United States Catholic Conference, 1986).

12. Martin Luther King, Jr., *A Testament of Hope: The Essential Speeches and Writings of Martin Luther King, Jr.,* ed. James M. Washington (San Francisco: HarperCollins, 1991), 105.

13. Ibid., 314.

14. James H. Cone, *Speaking the Truth* (Grand Rapids: William B. Eerdmans, 1986), vii.

15. Beverly Wildung Harrison, *Making the Connections: Essays in Feminist Theological Ethics* (Boston: Beacon Press, 1985), 22-41.

16. Gustavo Gutiérrez, *We Drink from Our Own Wells* (Maryknoll, N.Y.: Orbis Books, 1984).

17. National Conference of Catholic Bishops, *Economic Justice for All,* 21.

18. Richard B. Miller, ed., *War in the Twentieth Century: Sources in Theological Ethics* (Louisville: Westminster John Knox Press, 1992).

19. Joerg Rieger, *Remember the Poor: The Challenge to Theology in the Twenty-first Century* (Harrisburg, Penn.: Trinity Press International, 1998).

20. Niebuhr, *Love and Justice: Selections from the Shorter Writings of Reinhold Niebuhr,* ed. D. B. Robertson (Louisville: Westminster John Knox Press, 1992), 43. This essay was first published in 1934.

Index of Subjects and Authors

Index of Scripture References